GREAT WHISKEYS

SUNTORY
SINGLE MALT
WHISKY
AGED 12 YEARS
THE YAMAZAKI SINGLE MALT WHISKY
STRAIGHT
Rye
WHISKY
C.C.
20
山崎
43%vol. 70cl

Material previously published in *World Whiskey*

GREAT WHISKEYS

500 OF THE BEST FROM AROUND THE WORLD

EDITOR-IN-CHIEF **CHARLES MACLEAN**

LONDON, NEW YORK, MUNICH,
MELBOURNE, DELHI

US Editors Jenny Siklós, Shannon Beatty

DK INDIA
Editorial Manager Glenda Fernandes
Senior Art Editor (Lead) Navidita Thapa
DTP Manager Sunil Sharma
Designer Heema Sabharwal
DTP Designers Manish Chandra Upreti,
Mohammed Usman, Neeraj Bhatia

DK UK
Editor Shashwati Tia Sarkar
Designer Katherine Raj
Managing Editor Dawn Henderson
Managing Art Editor Marianne Markham
Senior Jacket Creative Nicola Powling
Production Editor Ben Marcus
Production Controller Dominika Szczepanska
Creative Technical Support Sonia Charbonnier

Material first published in the United States
in *World Whiskey*, 2009
This edition first published in 2011
by DK Publishing
375 Hudson Street
New York, New York 10014

11 12 13 10 9 8 7 6 5 4 3 2 1
001–179127–April/2011

Published in Great Britain by Dorling Kindersley Limited.

A catalog record for this book is available
from the Library of Congress.

ISBN 978-0-7566-7184-6

Printed and bound in Singapore by Star Standard

Discover more at **www.dk.com**

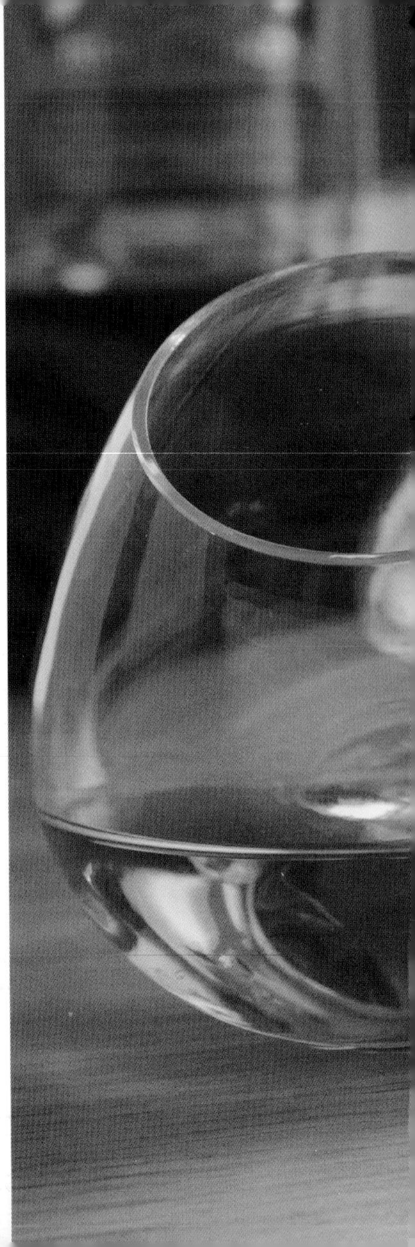

CONTENTS

INTRODUCTION

There's an old saying in Scotland: "There's no bad whisky. Just good whisky and better whisky." The whiskeys featured in this book come from all over the world. As you will see, great whiskey is now being made in South Asia, Australasia, and Europe, not just the "established" whiskey countries of Scotland, Ireland, the US, Canada, and Japan.

Whiskey is recognized as the most complex spirit on the planet. It is made from the simplest and most natural of ingredients—cereal grains, water, and yeast—yet the craft and tradition that goes into its making elevate it to the rank of "noble spirit," presenting a huge spectrum of aromas and tastes. Like people, every whiskey is different—each has its own personality. Some are big, bold, and rowdy; others delicate, elegant, and shy. Some you may not take to immediately may later become good friends. My selection has been guided by six of the world's leading whiskey writers—Dave Broom, Tom Bruce-Gardyne, Ian Buxton, Peter Mulryan, Hans Offringa, and Gavin D. Smith—and I am deeply grateful to them for writing up the individual entries.

How you choose to enjoy whiskey—with or without water or ice; with soda or lemonade; with ginger ale or cola—is a matter of personal preference. In China they like it with iced tea, in Brazil with coconut water. However "flavor" is not just about taste, it also embraces smell. Indeed, to truly appreciate the nuances of flavor in whiskey, particularly malt whiskey, you should add nothing but a dash of water, and present the drink in a glass that allows you to consider its aroma to the full.

Secreted within this listing of world whiskeys are tours that will guide you to whiskey regions of Scotland, Ireland, the US, and Japan. No experience adds more to the enjoyment of whiskey than visiting a working distillery, to savor the aromas, appreciate the skill, dedication, and time that goes into making this profound spirit, and of course, to sample a dram right at its source.

Maybe you are just setting out on this journey of discovery; perhaps you're well down the road to becoming a connoisseur. Either way, I hope this book will be a useful guide and will introduce you to some interesting flavors.

Explore and enjoy!

Charles MacLean

8PM

India
Owner: Radico Khaitan
www.radicokhaitan.com

Launched as recently as 1999, 8PM had the singular distinction of selling a million cases in its first year (it now sells 3 million). The brand owner is Radico Khaitan, based at Rampur Distillery, Uttar Pradesh. Established in 1943, it is now a gigantic unit with a capacity of over 20 million gallons (90 million liters) of alcohol a year.

The company owns other whiskey brands, including Whytehall, and it has recently formed a partnership with Diageo, the world's largest drinks conglomerate, to produce Masterstroke *(see p248)*.

◀ 8PM CLASSIC
BLEND
Made from "a mix of quality grains," this has a core that promises *"thaath"* (boldness, opulence) and "the reach of a man to the dream world."

8PM ROYALE
BLEND
A blend of Indian spirits and mature Scotch malt whiskies.

100 PIPERS

Scotland

Owner: Chivas Brothers

Created in 1965 by Seagram, and named after an old Scots song, 100 Pipers was originally a contender in the "value" sector of the Scotch whisky market, where it was an immediate success. The blend contains malts from Allt-a-Bhainne and Braeval (distilleries that mainly supply malts for blends), and probably some Glenlivet and Longmorn as well. Seagrams developed the brand very effectively and it has continued to prosper under the new owners, Chivas Brothers (themselves owned by Pernod Ricard). It is one of the bestselling whiskies in Thailand, a dynamic market for Scotch, and is growing rapidly in many countries, especially Spain, Venezuela, Australia, and India.

100 PIPERS ▶

BLEND 40% ABV

Pale in color. A light and very mixable whisky, with a smooth yet subtly smoky taste.

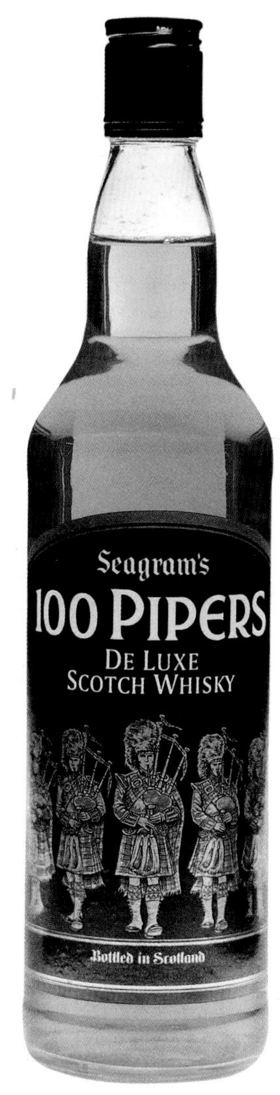

ABERFELDY

Scotland
Aberfeldy, Perthshire
www.dewarswow.com

Aberfeldy was built by John Dewar & Sons in 1898 to supply malts for the company's blends, but now also offers some single malt bottlings. Its life-long bond with Dewar's White Label is celebrated at its impressive, fully interactive visitor center, Dewar's World of Whisky, opened in 2000. Visitors see the rudiments of malt whisky distilling, but the main emphasis is on the art of blending and the role of Tommy Dewar (1864–1930), arguably the greatest whisky baron of them all.

◀ ABERFELDY 12-YEAR-OLD

SINGLE MALT: HIGHLANDS
40% ABV

The standard expression has a clean, apple-scented nose with a medium-bodied fruity character in the mouth.

ABERFELDY 21-YEAR-OLD

SINGLE MALT: HIGHLANDS
40% ABV

Launched in 2005, this has greater depth and richness than the 12-year-old, with a sweet, heathery nose and a slight spicy catch on the finish.

ABERLOUR

Scotland

Aberlour, Banffshire
www.aberlour.com

Aberlour's extreme popularity in France makes it one of the top ten bestselling malts in the world. As part of the old Campbell Distillers, it has been owned by the French group Pernod Ricard since 1975. Its malt is used in a great number of blends, particularly in Clan Campbell, but up to half the production is bottled as a single malt in a wide range of age statements and finishes.

ABERLOUR 12-YEAR-OLD SHERRY MATURED ▶

SINGLE MALT: SPEYSIDE
40% ABV

With its deep, reddish hue from new sherry wood, this expression has a nutty, fruitcake character and a creamy, buttery texture.

ABERLOUR A'BUNADH

SINGLE MALT: SPEYSIDE
60% ABV

A'bunadh *(a-boon-ahh)*, "the origin" in Gaelic, is a cask strength, non chill-filtered malt matured in Oloroso casks. It has a sumptuous character of fruitcake and spice.

ALBERTA

Canada

1521 34th Avenue Southeast,
Calgary, Alberta
Owner: Jim Beam

Alberta Distillery was founded in Calgary in 1946 to take advantage of the immense Canadian prairies and the fine Rocky Mountain water. Rye is at the heart of many Canadian whiskeys, and is predominant in Alberta. Maturing takes place in first-fill bourbon casks, or even in new white-oak casks. Other brands from Alberta include Tangle Ridge *(see p339)* and Windsor Canadian *(see p374)*.

◀ ALBERTA SPRINGS 10-YEAR-OLD

CANADIAN RYE 40% ABV

A sweet aroma, with rye bread and black pepper. The taste is very sweet, even somewhat cloying, becoming charred and caramelized.

ALBERTA PREMIUM

CANADIAN RYE 40% ABV

Described as "Special Mild Canadian Rye Whiskey." The aroma presents vanilla toffee, a hint of spice, light citric notes, and fruitiness. The taste is sweet above all, with stewed apples, plums, and marzipan.

AMERICAN SPIRIT

USA

Wild Turkey Distillery,
US Highway 62 East,
Lawrenceburg, Kentucky
www.wildturkeybourbon.com

American Spirit is distilled at the Wild Turkey Distillery *(see p368)* by Austin Nicholls & Co, and was introduced in September 2007. According to Eddie Russell, who developed this expression with his father, Master Distiller Jimmy Russell, the name "American Spirit" seemed to suggest itself.

AMERICAN SPIRIT 15-YEAR-OLD ▶

BOURBON 50% ABV

Richly aromatic and characterful on the nose and silky-smooth in the mouth, with vanilla, brittle toffee, molasses, stewed fruits, spice, and a little mint. The finish is lengthy and spicy, with gentle oak and a final menthol note.

AMRUT

India

Amrut Distilleries, 36 Sampangi Tank Road, Bangalore, Karnataka
www.amrutdistilleries.com

In Hindu mythology, the *amrut* was a golden pot containing the elixir of life. This family-owned Indian company focuses on innovation, quality, and transparency: they use barley grown in the Punjabi foothills of the Himalayas, malted in Jaipur, and distilled in small batches 3,000 ft (900 m) above sea level in Bangalore, where it is matured in ex-bourbon and new oak casks and bottled without chill-filtration.

◀ AMRUT INDIAN SINGLE MALT CASK STRENGTH

SINGLE MALT 61.9% ABV

Lightly fruity and cereal-like; bourbon casks introduce toffee. More woody, spicy, and malty with water. Similar in profile to a young Speyside malt.

AMRUT PEATED INDIAN SINGLE MALT

SINGLE MALT 62.78% ABV

Cereal and kippery smoke on the nose; oily, with salt and pepper. The taste is sweet and malty, with a whiff of smoke in the finish.

ANCIENT AGE

USA
Buffalo Trace,
1001 Wilkinson Boulevard,
Frankfort, Kentucky
www.buffalotrace.com

Ancient Age was, from 1969 to 1999, the name of what is now the Buffalo Trace Distillery *(see p66)*. The brand was introduced in the 1930s shortly after the end of Prohibition, initially being distilled in Canada. After World War II, it was reformulated as a straight Kentucky-made bourbon, and went on to become one of the best-known brands produced by its proprietors.

ANCIENT AGE 10-YEAR-OLD ▶
BOURBON 40% ABV
This 10-year-old bourbon is complex and fragrant on the nose, with spices, fudge, oranges, and honey. It is medium-bodied and, after a slightly dry opening, the oily palate sweetens, developing vanilla and cocoa flavors, and a lightly charred note.

ANCNOC

Scotland

Knockdhu Distillery, Knock, Huntly, Aberdeenshire
www.ancnoc.com

Named after the nearby "Black Hill," the springs of which supply its water, anCnoc is the core expression of Knockdhu Distillery.

Historically significant for being the first distillery built by the Distillers Company Limited (DCL), Knockdhu's new owner, Inver House, has kept the character of the distillery. The traditional worm tubs for condensing the spirit add a slightly sulfury, meaty character to the new make.

◄ ANCNOC 1991
SINGLE MALT: SPEYSIDE
46% ABV
Vanilla, toffee, and wood on the nose. Fruity and full-bodied, with a hint of peatiness.

ANCNOC 12-YEAR-OLD
SINGLE MALT: SPEYSIDE
40% ABV
A relatively full-bodied Speyside malt, with notes of lemon peel and heather-honey on the nose, a fairly luscious mouthfeel, and some length on the finish.

ANGUS DUNDEE

Scotland
www.angusdundee.co.uk

With more than 50 years' experience in producing, blending, bottling, and distributing top-quality spirits, Angus Dundee is one of the few remaining truly independent family-owned companies in the Scotch whisky industry. It has two malt distilleries—Tomintoul and Glencadam—but is better known for its blending and broking activities. Other company-owned blends include Parkers and Scottish Royal.

THE DUNDEE ▶
BLEND 40% ABV
Hints of orange peel in a malty, medium-weight nose. There are some traces of smoke and some sweetness. Smooth on the palate.

OLD DUNDEE 12-YEAR-OLD
BLEND 43% ABV
Richer than its younger counterpart, with a longer finish. Orange notes develop into candied-peel. Soft in the mouth, and an elegant palate. There's a sugary tart flavor, but it's not cloying.

THE ANTIQUARY

Scotland
Owner: Tomatin Distillery
www.antiquary.co.uk

Introduced in 1857 and named after a novel by Sir Walter Scott, The Antiquary was a prized luxury blend in its heyday. Befitting its deluxe status, it has at its heart a very high malt-to-grain ratio, including some of the finest malts from Speyside and Highland distilleries and more than a splash of Tomatin. Islay seems to feature more strongly than previously.

◀ THE ANTIQUARY 12-YEAR-OLD

BLEND 40% ABV

Subtle fruitiness concealing a hint of apples. Outstanding smoothness, depth of flavor, and a long aftertaste. Other tasters have reported a striking peat influence, new to the blend.

THE ANTIQUARY 21-YEAR-OLD

BLEND 43% ABV

The subtle maltiness with muted peaty notes allows the heather, dandelion, and blackcurrant notes to flourish. A dash of Islay malt creates a truly exceptional dram: well-balanced, rich, and smooth. A stand-out blend that deserves to be more widely enjoyed.

ARDBEG

Scotland
Port Ellen, Islay
www.ardbeg.com

If Islay is the spiritual home of Scotland's pungent, peat-smoked whiskies, then Ardbeg is undoubtedly one of the island's leading disciples. The distillery was first licensed in 1815 in the parish of Kildalton, on Islay's southern coast just beyond Lagavulin and Laphroaig.

Reliance on the blending market left Ardbeg in a vulnerable position, however, and when "the whisky loch" became full to the brim in the early 1980s, the distillery was mothballed. ☛

ARDBEG 10-YEAR-OLD ▶
SINGLE MALT: ISLAY 46% ABV
This non chill-filtered malt has notes of creosote, tar, and smoked fish on the nose. Any sweetness on the tongue quickly dries to a smoky finish.

ARDBEG AIRIGH NAM BEIST
SINGLE MALT: ISLAY 46% ABV
A rich, spicy malt sweetened with vanilla notes from 16 years in bourbon casks. The name, pronounced *arry-nam -bayst*, means "shelter of the beast."

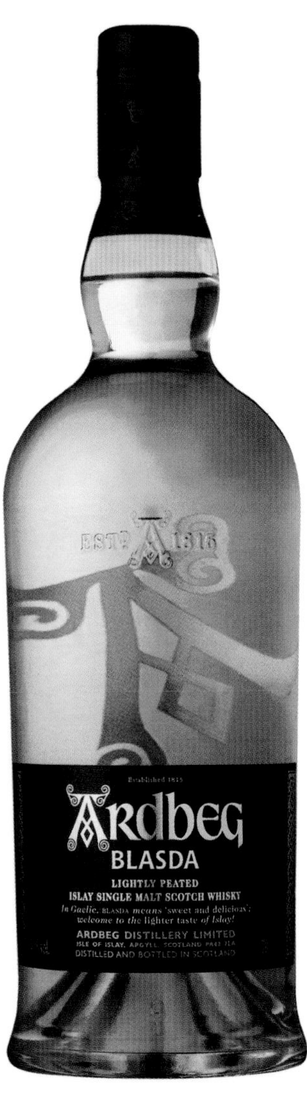

ARDBEG

In 1997, Ardbeg was rescued by Glenmorangie, who paid a reported £7m and then spent a further £1.4m on upgrading the distillery. At first, the years of non-production caused problems but, as the gaps in the inventory receded, the distillery was finally able to release a standard 10-year-old bottling. Since then, there has been a raft of new bottlings, which have added to Ardbeg's growing cult status among fans of Islay's smoky malt whiskies.

◀ ARDBEG BLASDA

SINGLE MALT: ISLAY 40% ABV

The Gaelic name translates as "sweet and delicious," a reference to a much gentler style than usual, made from malt peated at only 8ppm, one-third Ardbeg's usual levels.

ARDBEG UIGEADAIL

SINGLE MALT: ISLAY 54.2% ABV

Named after Loch Uigeadail—Ardbeg's water source—this has a deep gold color and a molasseslike sweetness on the nose, with savory, smoky notes following through on the tongue.

ARDMORE

Scotland
Kennethmont, Aberdeenshire
www.ardmorewhisky.com

Ardmore owes its existence to Teacher's Highland Cream *(see p341)*. The Teacher's blend was well-established in Scotland, particularly in Glasgow, where it was sold through Teacher's Dram Shops, and sales were growing abroad. To keep up with demand, Adam Teacher decided to build a new distillery in 1898 and found the ideal spot near Kennethmont, beside the main Aberdeen-to-Inverness railroad. Famed for producing the smokiest malt on Speyside, Ardmore released a 12-year-old in 1999 to celebrate its centenary. In 2005 the distillery became part of Fortune Brands.

ARDMORE TRADITIONAL CASK ▶
SINGLE MALT: SPEYSIDE
46% ABV
A smooth, relatively full-bodied malt, where the sweet American oak flavors from the cask are balanced by the dry, earthy character from the peat.

ARMORIK

France

Distillerie Warenghem, Route de Guingamp, 22300 Lannion, Bretagne
www.distillerie-warenghem.com

The Warenghem Distillery was founded in 1900 to produce apple cider and fruit spirits. It was not until 99 years later that the owners decided to start making other types of spirits, including malted beers and whiskey. There are now two types of whiskey made here: Armorik, a single malt, and WB (Whiskey Breton), a blend. The type of casks used for maturation is not specified.

◀ **ARMORIK WHISKEY BRETON**
SINGLE MALT 40% ABV
A young spirit, Armorik is fresh and very spicy, with a salty tang and a dry, oaky influence in the finish.

ARRAN

Scotland

Lochranza, Isle of Arran
www.arranwhisky.com

When the distillery opened in 1993, it marked the return of distilling on the Isle of Arran after a hiatus of some 156 years. Arran takes its water from Loch na Davie on the island's north coast, and the island itself is positioned in the Gulf Stream, where the warm waters and climate system are said to beneficially speed up the maturation period. Arran creates a range of blends named for Robert Burns, who was born nearby on the mainland *(see p301)*.

ARRAN 10-YEAR-OLD ▶

SINGLE MALT: ISLANDS
46% ABV

Bottled without chill-filtering, this has fresh bread and vanilla aromas, with citrus notes that carry through onto the tongue.

ARRAN 12-YEAR-OLD

SINGLE MALT: ISLANDS
46% ABV

This expression has an orange peel and chocolate sweetness and a rich, creamy texture thanks to the influence of sherry wood.

AUCHENTOSHAN

Scotland
Dalmuir, Clydebank, Glasgow
www.auchentoshan.co.uk

While Glenkinchie sits just south of Edinburgh, Scotland's other main Lowlands distillery lies west of Glasgow by the Erskine Bridge and the Clyde River.

Auchentoshan, licensed in 1823, produced a modest 50,000 gallons (225,000 liters) a year with a single pair of stills until it acquired a third still. Ever since, Auchentoshan, with its triple-distilled malt, has been almost unique in Scotland. This being the

◄ AUCHENTOSHAN CLASSIC
SINGLE MALT: LOWLANDS
40% ABV
With no age statement, this is a young introduction to the Auchentoshan range, with lots of vanilla sweetness and citrus.

AUCHENTOSHAN 12-YEAR-OLD
SINGLE MALT: LOWLANDS
40% ABV
This expression replaced the old 10-year-old and has a dense, spicy character thanks to the use of sherry casks.

standard style of Irish whiskey, it soon caught on among the burgeoning Irish community in Glasgow.

The Clydebank area was a key target for the Luftwaffe in World War II and, after some heavy bombing in 1941, Auchentoshan has since drawn its cooling water from a pond created in a giant bomb crater.

Auchentoshan joined forces with the Islay distillery Bowmore in 1984, becoming Morrison Bowmore, now part Suntory. In the past decade, the range of single malts has been greatly expanded.

AUCHENTOSHAN THREE WOOD ▶
SINGLE MALT: LOWLANDS
43% ABV

This is matured in three different types of cask, and sherry clearly has a big influence on the color and sweet, candied-fruit flavors.

AUCHENTOSHAN 18-YEAR-OLD
SINGLE MALT: LOWLANDS
43% ABV

This is a classic nutty, spicy malt with plenty of age and complexity on the palate and some fruity sherry notes on the nose.

AUCHROISK

Scotland
Mulben, Banffshire
www.malts.com

This modern distillery lies on the main road between Craigellachie and Keith. The site was bought by International Distillers & Vintners (IDV)—now merged with Diageo—in 1970 for £5m, and Auchroisk (which means "ford of the red stream" in Gaelic) was up and running four years later. The principal role of the distillery was to supply malt for the J&B blend, but, after a decade, it was decided to release a distillery bottling as well. This was called the Singleton of Auchroisk. The name was soon abandoned, however, and replaced by a 10-year-old in the Flora & Fauna range and occasional Rare Malt series bottlings.

◀ AUCHROISK FLORA & FAUNA 10-YEAR-OLD
SINGLE MALT: SPEYSIDE
43% ABV

An aromatic Speyside with a wisp of smoke and citrus notes, combined with malty flavors that dry on the finish.

AULTMORE

Scotland
Keith, Banffshire

Alexander Edward was a seasoned distiller at Benrinnes before establishing the Craigellachie Distillery with Peter Mackie, the whisky baron and founder of the White Horse blend. In 1895, at the peak of the late-Victorian whisky boom, Edward built Aultmore, his third distillery, on the flat farmland between Keith and the sea. After acquisition by John Dewar & Sons and DCL, the distillery was one of five sold to Bacardi in 1998.

AULTMORE FLORA & FAUNA 12-YEAR-OLD ▶

SINGLE MALT: SPEYSIDE
40% ABV

The main distillery bottling is a crisp, herbal, aperitif-style malt with a gentle, perfumed nose and a malty flavor that dries on the finish.

AULTMORE SINGLE MALTS OF SCOTLAND 15-YEAR-OLD

SINGLE MALT: SPEYSIDE
46% ABV

This older expression has a floral, nutty, spicy aroma coupled with a trace of chocolate. It is medium-to full-bodied and luscious in texture.

BAGPIPER

India
Owner: United Spirits
www.unitedspirits.in

"The World's No.1 Non-Scotch Whiskey" sells nearly 14 million cases a year. An IMFL (Indian Made Foreign Liquor), probably made from molasses alcohol and concentrates, it was launched by the United Spirits subsidiary Herbertson's in 1987 and, in its first year, sold 100,000 cases. The brand has always been closely associated with Bollywood, India's huge film-production industry, and has successfully won accreditation from many movie stars. The company also broadcasts a weekly *Bagpiper* show on TV, and is a sponsor of talent-spotting programs.

◀ BAGPIPER GOLD
BLEND 42.8% ABV
Gold is the premium expression of Bagpiper, but it still has a somewhat artificial taste and is best drunk with a mixer like cola.

BAILIE NICOL JARVIE

Scotland
Owner: Glenmorangie

Produced by Glenmorangie, Bailie Nicol Jarvie—or BNJ as it is commonly called in Scotland—is reputed to contain a healthy measure of both Glenmorangie and Glen Moray single malts. In fact, it has one of the highest malt contents of any blended whisky. It is excellent value and has gained something of a cult following, its adherents savoring the idea of being one of the cognoscenti, perhaps, for it is not at all heavily promoted. The label has a satisfying period feel.

BAILIE NICOL JARVIE ▸
BLEND 40% ABV
Smooth, subtle, and full of character, with a delicate balance of sweet Speyside, aromatic Highland, and peaty Islay malt whiskies blended with only the finest grain whisky.

BAKER'S

USA

Jim Beam Distillery,
149 Happy Hollow Road,
Clermont, Kentucky
www.jimbeam.com

Baker's is one of three whiskeys that were introduced in 1992 as Beam's Small Batch Bourbon Collection. It is named after Baker Beam, the former Clermont Master Distiller and grand-nephew of the legendary Jim Beam himself. He is also a cousin of the late Booker Noe, the high-profile distiller who instigated small-batch bourbon distilling. Baker Beam's namesake whiskey is distilled using the standard Jim Beam formula, but is aged for longer and offered at a higher bottling strength.

◀ **BAKER'S 7-YEAR-OLD**
BOURBON 53.5% ABV
Baker's is a fruity, toasty expression of the Jim Beam formula: medium-bodied, mellow, and richly flavored, with notes of vanilla and caramel.

BAKERY HILL

Australia
28 Ventnor Street,
North Balwyn, Victoria
www.bakeryhilldistillery.com.au

David Baker, chemist and founder of Bakery Hill Distillery, was determined to prove that top-quality malt whiskey could be made in Australia. He has succeeded: his single cask, non chill-filtered malts are already winning awards. At the moment, however, they are only available from the distillery, near Melbourne, Victoria.

The barley strains Australian Franklin and Australian Schooner are sourced locally and sometimes malted over locally cut peat.

BAKERY HILL CASK STRENGTH PEATED MALT ▶

SINGLE MALT 59.88% ABV

Intense peatiness on the nose, with dark cherry. The taste is sweet (toffee, honeycomb), with some salt and smoke. It has a good texture.

BAKERY HILL PEATED MALT

SINGLE MALT 46% ABV

A sweet and oaky balance of peat and malt on the nose. These aromas carry through in the taste.

BALBLAIR

Scotland
Edderton, Tain, Ross-shire
www.balblair.com

Founded in 1790 by John Ross, Balblair is one of only a handful of 18th-century distilleries that has survived to this day. It remained in family hands for over 100 years. Since 1996, the distillery has been owned by Inver House Distillers, who began with a core range called Elements. This was succeeded by a range of vintage malts in a similar style to The Glenrothes bottlings, right down to the bulbous bottle shape.

◀ **BALBLAIR 75**
SINGLE MALT: HIGHLANDS
46% ABV
The sherry-matured vintage expression has a distinct rum-raisin character, with notes of butterscotch and some underlying fruit flavors that taper to a long finish.

BALBLAIR 89
SINGLE MALT: HIGHLANDS
43% ABV
Matured mainly in ex-bourbon casks, this has a slightly sweeter nose than the 75, with notes of candy apple, tropical fruits, and vanilla ice cream.

BALLANTINE'S

Scotland
www.ballantines.com

Ballantine's was a pioneer in developing aged blends. Its range is arguably the most extensive in the world today, and includes Ballantine's Finest (the standard bottling), as well as Ballantine's 12-year-old, 17-year-old, 21-year-old, and 30-year-old. The range is the world's second biggest Scotch whisky by volume and the top-selling super-premium brand in Asia.

The blend is noted for its complexity, with over 40 different malts and grains being used. The two Speyside single malts ☛

BALLANTINE'S FINEST ▶
BLEND 40% ABV
A sweet, soft-textured blend, with the Speyside malts giving chocolate, vanilla, and apple notes.

BALLANTINE'S 12-YEAR-OLD
BLEND 40% ABV
Golden-hued, with a honey sweetness on the nose, and vanilla from the oak. Creamy texture and balanced palate, with floral, honey, and oaky vanilla notes. Some tasters detect a hint of salt.

BALLANTINE'S

Glenburgie and Miltonduff form the base for the blend, but malts from all parts of Scotland are also employed. For maturation, Ballantine's principally favors the use of ex-bourbon barrels, for the vanilla influences and sweet creamy notes they characteristically bring to the blend.

The Glenburgie Distillery has been completely remodeled and modernized and is today Ballantine's spiritual home.

◀ BALLANTINE'S 21-YEAR-OLD
BLEND 43% ABV
The sought-after older expressions of Ballantine's are deep in color, with traces of heather, smoke, licorice, and spice on the nose. The 21-year-old has a complex, balanced palate, with sherry, honey, and floral notes.

BALLANTINE'S 17-YEAR-OLD
BLEND 43% ABV
A deep, balanced, and elegant whisky with a hint of wood and vanilla. The body is full and creamy, with a vibrant, honeyed sweetness and hints of oak and peat smoke on the palate.

BALMENACH

Scotland
Cromdale, Grantown-on-Spey, Morayshire
www.inverhouse.com

In 1824 James McGregor, like many illicit distillers, decided to come in from the cold and take out a license for his farm distillery near Grantown-on-Spey. It was owned by the family for 100 years until they sold out to DCL. Aside from during World War II, the distillery was in constant production until 1993, when its whisky was available as part of the Flora & Fauna range. In 1997, Balmenach was sold to Inver House, who fired up the stills the following year. A full distillery bottling has had to wait, owing to a dearth of inherited stocks.

BALMENACH GORDON & MACPHAIL 1990 ▶

SINGLE MALT: SPEYSIDE
43% ABV

Citrus, grass, and malt on the nose, slight smoke on the palate. Opens up with water.

BALVENIE

Scotland

Dufftown, Keith, Banffshire
www.thebalvenie.com

Within six years of setting up Glenfiddich in 1886, William Grant was converting Balvenie New House (a derelict Georgian pile) next door into another distillery using second-hand stills. This expansion was partly a result of a request from an Aberdeen blender who desperately needed 400 gallons (1,800 liters) of Glenlivet-style whisky a week.

◀ THE BALVENIE DOUBLEWOOD 12-YEAR-OLD

SINGLE MALT: SPEYSIDE
40% ABV

After a decade in American oak, Doublewood spends two years in ex-sherry casks to give it a smooth, confected, slightly nutty character.

THE BALVENIE SIGNATURE 12-YEAR-OLD

SINGLE MALT: SPEYSIDE
40% ABV

A vatting of three types of cask—sherry, first-fill bourbon, and refill bourbon—which give a mix of confected fruit and vanilla with a syrupy texture.

Although physically dwarfed by Glenfiddich, Balvenie is no boutique distillery: it can produce 1.4 million gallons (6.4 million liters) a year and has built up an impressive range of single malts. As an artisan distillery, it grows some of its own barley, in contrast to Glenfiddich. It has also retained its floor maltings to satisfy part of its requirements, and employs a coppersmith and a team of coopers. Indeed, Balvenie's attention to maturation and different wood finishes rivals even that of Glenmorangie.

THE BALVENIE SINGLE BARREL 15-YEAR-OLD ▶

SINGLE MALT: SPEYSIDE
47.8% ABV

This 15-year-old is bottled one cask at a time, so each is subtly different from the last, although sharing a sweet woody character and nutty flavor.

THE BALVENIE VINTAGE CASK 1976

SINGLE MALT: SPEYSIDE
53.8% ABV

Autumnal wet leaves and damp, woody aromas. Heavy tannins on the palate, balanced by fruitiness; slightly sweet in the finish.

BARTON

USA

Tom Moore Distillery, 1 Barton Road, Bardstown, Kentucky

The Tom Moore Distillery in Bardstown, Nelson County makes what were formerly known as the Barton brand whiskeys. Bardstown is in the true heartland of bourbon, and once boasted more than 20 distilleries. The whiskeys made at Tom Moore are typically youthful, dry, and aromatic.

In 2009, the Sazerac Company Inc., which also owns Buffalo Trace, acquired the Tom Moore Distillery from Constellation Brands, as well as all the Barton whiskeys produced there, including Very Old Barton, Kentucky Gentleman *(see p211)*, Ridgemont *(see p299)*, Kentucky Tavern, Ten High, and Tom Moore.

◄ **VERY OLD BARTON**

BOURBON 43% ABV

Six years is comparatively old for a Barton whiskey, hence its name. The nose is rich, syrupy, and spicy, with a prickle of salt. Big-bodied in the mouth, it is fruity and spicy, with spices and ginger in the drying finish.

BASIL HAYDEN'S

USA

Jim Beam Distillery,
149 Happy Hollow Road,
Clermont, Kentucky
www.jimbeam.com

Basil Hayden's was one of the three whiskeys that made up Beam's pioneering Small Batch Bourbon Collection, introduced in 1992. Basil Hayden was an early Kentucky settler from Maryland who began making whiskey in the late-18th century near Bardstown, and it is claimed that the recipe for this particular expression dates from that period.

BASIL HAYDEN'S 8-YEAR-OLD ▶

BOURBON 40% ABV

The nose is light, aromatic, and spicy, with flavors of soft rye, wood-polish, spices, pepper, vanilla, and a hint of honey on the comparatively dry palate. The finish is long, with notes of peppery rye.

THE BELGIAN OWL

Belgium
The Owl Distillery, Rue Sainte Anne 94, B4460 Grâce-Hollogne
www.belgianwhiskey.com

Master Distiller Etienne Bouillon founded this distillery in the French-speaking part of Belgium in 2004. He uses home-grown barley and first-fill bourbon casks to produce a 3-year-old single malt whiskey. The first batch was bottled in the fall of 2007. The Belgian Owl Distillery was formerly known under the names Lambicool and PUR.E.

◀ **BELGIAN SINGLE MALT**
SINGLE MALT 46% ABV
This non chill-filtered malt offers vanilla, coconut, banana, and ice cream, topped with fig, followed by a crescendo of other flavors such as lemon, apples, and ginger. A long finish, with ripe fruits and vanilla.

BELL'S

Scotland
www.bellswhisky.co.za

"Several fine whiskies blended together please the palates of a greater number of people than one whisky unmixed," wrote the first Arthur Bell.

In keeping with this spirit, the current owners of Bell's, Diageo, lay great emphasis on the skill of the blenders. Bell's acquired Blair Athol (the source of the single malt at the heart of the blend) and Dufftown distilleries in 1933, adding Inchgower in 1936. The blend always evolves: the company insists that, in blind taste tests, drinkers prefer the new version.

BELL'S ORIGINAL ▶
BLEND 40% ABV
As well as Blair Athol, Dufftown and Inchgower are important components here, along with Glenkinchie and Caol Ila. Medium-bodied blend, with a nutty aroma and a lightly spiced flavor.

BELL'S SPECIAL RESERVE
BLEND 40% ABV
Special Reserve has smoky hints from the Islay malts, tempered with warm pepper and a rich honey complexity.

BEN NEVIS

Scotland
Lochy Bridge, Fort William
www.bennevisdistillery.com

Scotland's most northerly west coast distillery was founded in 1825 by "Long John" Macdonald, who was the inspiration for the once-popular blend of that name *(see p238)*. Sitting by Loch Linnhe, Fort William, the 19th century distillery even had its own small fleet of steamers to ferry the whisky down the loch.

Periodic closures during the 1970s and 80s have caused gaps in its inventory, but despite this, a number of older single malts have been released alongside the various Dew of Ben Nevis blends. The 10-year-old is the only regular distillery bottling, although single-cask and wood-finished releases appear occasionally. Various independent bottlings have also been released.

◀ BEN NEVIS 10-YEAR-OLD
SINGLE MALT: HIGHLANDS
46% ABV
A big, mouth-filling West Highlands malt with a sweet smack of oak and an oily texture that finishes dry.

BENRIACH

Scotland
Longmorn, Elgin, Morayshire
www.benriachdistillery.co.uk

Of all the Speyside distilleries built on the crest of the great speculative wave of whisky-making at the end of the 19th century, few crashed so badly as BenRiach. It opened in 1897 but only operated until 1903, when it was closed for the first half of the 20th century. Then, in 1965, after a major refurbishment, its pair of stills was fired up again. Its subsequent owners, Seagram, having no distillery on Islay, decided to ☛

BENRIACH 12-YEAR-OLD ▶
SINGLE MALT: SPEYSIDE
40% ABV

More classically Speyside in character than the 10-year-old, with a heathery nose, creamy vanilla ice cream flavor, and a hint of honey.

BENRIACH CURIOSITAS 10-YEAR-OLD
SINGLE MALT: SPEYSIDE
40% ABV

A bitter-sweet whisky with a dense peaty flavor. Beneath the smoke, there are flavors of tea cookies, cereal, and some citrus notes.

BENRIACH

☛ produce a powerful peat-smoked malt at BenRiach in 1983. There were still some stocks of this peated BenRiach left when a South African consortium led by Billy Walker took over in 2004 from Chivas Brothers. This led to the Curiositas and Authenticus bottlings—the only commercially available Speyside single malts distilled from peated malted barley.

With 5,000 different casks dating back to 1970 and different levels of peating to play with, Billy Walker has dramatically expanded the range of BenRiach malts available, although he has quite some way to go if he wants to rival Bruichladdich's 200-plus releases.

◀ BENRIACH 16-YEAR-OLD

SINGLE MALT: SPEYSIDE
40% ABV

A nutty, spicy Speysider, with a honeyed texture in the mouth and perhaps the faintest wisp of smoke.

BENRIACH 20-YEAR-OLD

SINGLE MALT: SPEYSIDE
40% ABV

The long years in oak have given this expression a dry, woody flavor, with sharp citrus notes and a clean finish.

BENRINNES

Scotland
Aberlour, Banffshire
www.malts.com

The original Benrinnes Distillery was founded in 1826 at Whitehouse Farm on lower Speyside by Peter McKenzie, but was swept away in a flood three years later. In 1834 a new distillery called the Lyne of Ruthrie was built a few miles away and, despite bankruptcies and a bad fire in 1896, it has survived as Benrinnes. What you see today is a modern post-war distillery, which was completely rebuilt in the mid-1950s. It has six stills that operate a partial form of triple distillation, with one wash still paired with two spirit stills.

BENRINNES FLORA & FAUNA 15-YEAR-OLD ▶
SINGLE MALT: SPEYSIDE
43% ABV
The only official distillery bottling is fairly sumptuous, with some smoke and spicy flavors and a creamy mouthfeel.

BENROMACH

Scotland
Forres, Morayshire
www.benromach.com

With just a single pair of stills and a maximum production of 110,000 gallons (500,000 liters) of pure alcohol a year, Benromach was always something of a pint-sized distillery. It was founded in 1898 and changed hands no fewer than six times in its first 100 years. At one point, it found itself part of National Distillers of America, sharing a stable with bourbon brands such as Old Crow and Old Grand-Dad.

◀ BENROMACH TRADITIONAL
SINGLE MALT: SPEYSIDE
40% ABV
This expression has a clean, light, floral character with a gentle phenolic edge and a trace of caramel.

BENROMACH CASK STRENGTH 1981
SINGLE MALT: SPEYSIDE
54.2% ABV
The nose is quite closed at first, but with water it opens up to reveal ripe orchard fruits and notes of cinnamon and sherry trifle.

Then, like so many dispossessed distilleries, Benromach became part of the giant DCL who, as UDV, mothballed the distillery in 1983, along with many others. This time the stills were ripped out and the warehouses knocked down, and it seemed Benromach would never produce whisky again.

Benromach's savior was the famous firm of independent bottlers Gordon & MacPhail of Elgin, who bought the distillery in 1993. A new pair of stills was installed, and the first spirit flowed from it in 1999, when Prince Charles officially opened the new Benromach.

BENROMACH 25-YEAR-OLD ▶
SINGLE MALT: SPEYSIDE
43% ABV

The bourbon-cask brother to the sherried Vintage. Mellow, soft in the mouth, with a fruity citrus character.

BENROMACH ORIGINS
SINGLE MALT: SPEYSIDE
50% ABV

Origins is a new series. Batch 1 Golden Promise is named for the strain of barley used. Maturation is in first- and second-fill sherry casks.

BERNHEIM

USA

Heaven Hill Distillery,
1701 West Breckinridge Street,
Louisville, Kentucky
www.bernheimwheatwhiskey.com

The Bernheim brand takes its name from Heaven Hill's Bernheim Distillery in Louisville, Kentucky, where Heaven Hill whiskeys have been produced since the plant was acquired in 1999. Launched in 2005, Bernheim is the only straight wheat whiskey on the US market.

Heaven Hill father and son Master Distillers Parker and Craig Beam developed the wheat formula with a minimum of 51 percent winter wheat, and the recipe also includes corn and malted barley.

◀ **BERNHEIM ORIGINAL**
WHEAT WHISKEY 45% ABV
Bernheim exhibits light fruit notes on the spicy nose, with freshly sawn wood, toffee, vanilla, sweetish grain, and a hint of mint on the palate. A long, elegant, honeyed, and spicy finish.

BLACK & WHITE

Scotland
Owner: Diageo

A fondly regarded brand from the Buchanan's stable, Black & White originally went by the name Buchanan's Special. The story goes that, in the 1890s, James Buchanan supplied his whisky to the House of Commons in a very dark bottle with a white label. Apparently incapable of memorizing the name, British parliamentarians simply called for "Black and White." Buchanan adopted the name and subsequently adorned the label with two dogs—a black Scottish terrier and a white West Highland terrier. Today it is marketed by Diageo in France, Brazil, and Venezuela, where it continues to enjoy a popularity long since lost in its homeland.

BLACK & WHITE ▶
BLEND 40% ABV
A high-class, traditional-style blend. Layered hints of peat, smoke, and oak.

BLACK BOTTLE

Scotland
Owner: Burn Stewart Distillers

Burn Stewart Distillers have made great efforts to invest in the blend quality of Black Bottle, and many commentators agree that the blend profile now resembles that of the original, created in 1879.

At the time of writing, the excellent 10-year-old expression is due to be discontinued. This is a quality blend to taste before supplies dry up.

◄ BLACK BOTTLE
BLEND 40% ABV
Black Bottle contains malt from seven Islay distilleries, along with hefty helpings of the company's Deanston malt. The nose is fresh and fruity, with hints of peat, while the palate is full, with a slightly honeyed sweetness followed by a distinctive, smoky flavor. The finish is long and warming, with a smoky Islay character.

BLACK BOTTLE 10-YEAR-OLD
BLEND 40% ABV
Like the original blend, the 10-year-old contains malt from seven Islay distilleries, but this expression is richer and more rounded.

BLACK DOG

Scotland
Owner: Whyte & Mackay

Walter Millard, a Scot trading from Calcutta, was looking for a blended Scotch to sell in India. In 1883, after some research, he appointed Charles Mackinlay & Co. (now part of Whyte & Mackay) to make up the blend. As an eager fisherman, he named it Black Dog after a favorite salmon fly. Black Dog was re-introduced to India in 2006. The following year, United Spirits, the largest distiller in India, bought Whyte & Mackay.

BLACK DOG CENTENARY ▶
BLEND 40% ABV
Sweet malt, light butterscotch, and cream, with light herbal notes on the nose. A firm body, with malt, oak, dark chocolate, and caramel in the mouth.

BLACK VELVET

Canada
2925 9th Avenue North,
Lethbridge, Alberta
www.blackvelvetwhisky.com

Black Velvet is the third bestselling Canadian whiskey in the US. It was created by Gilbey Canada in the 1950s as Black Label, and made at the Old Palliser Distillery in Toronto. It was so successful that, in 1973, the Black Velvet Distillery was established at Lethbridge, in the shadow of the Rockies, only a couple of hours drive from the US border. In 1999, both Black Velvet and Palliser were sold to Barton Brands, then later became part of Constellation Brands.

◀ BLACK VELVET RESERVE
BLEND 40% ABV
A light and mellow nose with vanilla notes. The palate is mild and sweet, with butterscotch, a faint citrus note, and light spiciness. Velvet-smooth texture, but the flavor lacks depth.

BLADNOCH

Scotland
Bladnoch, Wigtown, Wigtonshire
www.bladnoch.co.uk

Scotland's most southerly distillery was bought and sold several times over the 20th century, spending long periods lying idle in between. Finally, Guinness UDV (now Diageo) sold it to Raymond Armstrong from Northern Ireland in 1994. The deal brokered was that Bladnoch would never produce whisky again but, Diageo relented in 2000 and the distillery is now allowed to produce 250,000 bottles a year. Occasional older bottlings and a Flora & Fauna release can be found. Bladnoch will also sell you whisky by the cask.

BLADNOCH 15-YEAR-OLD ▶
SINGLE MALT: LOWLANDS
55% ABV
A light, crisp, aperitif-style whisky with a trace of green apples.

BLADNOCH 18-YEAR-OLD
SINGLE MALT: LOWLANDS
55% ABV
This smooth Lowland malt is bottled at full cask strength without chill-filtration, but is in short supply.

BLAIR ATHOL

Scotland
Pitlochry, Perthshire
www.malts.com

In 1798 John Stewart and Robert Robertson took out a license for their Aldour Distillery on the edge of Pitlochry. In an area crawling with illicit stills, life was tough for legitimate, tax-paying distilleries, and Aldour soon closed. It was resurrected in 1826 by Alexander Connacher, who renamed it Blair Athol. Within 30 years, some of the malt was being sold to the Perth blender Arthur Bell & Sons, who finally bought the distillery in 1933 *(see p41)*. Except for the 12-year-old and the occasional rare malt, nearly every drop goes into blends, particularly Bell's.

◀ BLAIR ATHOL FLORA & FAUNA 12-YEAR-OLD
SINGLE MALT: HIGHLANDS
43% ABV
Smooth, well-rounded flavors, with spice and candied fruit, and a trace of smoke on the finish.

BLANTON'S

USA

Buffalo Trace,
1001 Wilkinson Boulevard,
Frankfort, Kentucky
www.buffalotrace.com

Colonel Albert Bacon Blanton worked for no fewer than 55 years at what is now the Buffalo Trace Distillery, starting as office boy in 1897 and graduating to distillery manager in 1912. When he retired in 1955, the distillery was renamed Blanton's in his honor. This single barrel expression was created in 1984 by Master Distiller Elmer T. Lee, who worked with Blanton during the 1950s.

BLANTON'S SINGLE BARREL ▸
BOURBON 46.5% ABV
The nose of Blanton's is soft, with toffee, leather, and a hint of mint. Full-bodied and rounded on the palate, this is a notably sweet bourbon, embracing vanilla, caramel, honey, and spices. The finish is long and creamy, with a hint of late spice.

BLENDERS PRIDE

India

Owner: Pernod Ricard
www.pernod-ricard.com

Since it fell under the ownership of Pernod Ricard, this brand has been neck and neck with Royal Challenge *(see p305)* as the bestseller in its sector. It is a premium IMFL (Indian Made Foreign Liquor, made from Scotch malts and Indian grains), whose name comes from a story about the master blenders who exposed a cask of whiskey to the warmth of the sun at regular intervals. The delicate sweetness and aromatic flavor of the blend are testimony to the success of their experiment.

◀ **BLENDERS PRIDE**
BLEND 42.8% ABV
A smooth and rich mouthfeel, with a sweet taste that gives way to a disappointingly dull finish.

BOOKER'S

USA

Jim Beam Distillery,
149 Happy Hollow Road,
Clermont, Kentucky
www.jimbeam.com

A brand created by the global Jim Beam company, Booker's is named after Jim Beam's grandson, Booker Noe. It is made to the same Jim Beam formula as Baker's *(see p30)*, and is still bottled unfiltered and undiluted to maintain its natural barrel flavors.

BOOKER'S KENTUCKY STRAIGHT ▶

BOURBON 60.5–63.5% ABV

Big, fruity, and spicy on the nose, Booker's is sweet and slightly nutty on the palate, with heat and spiciness in the oaky finish. A big, traditional, classy bourbon.

BOWMORE

Scotland

Bowmore, Isle of Islay
www.bowmore.co.uk

The oldest surviving distillery on Islay was founded in 1779. The distillery remained small for years, until the Glasgow firm of W. & J. Mutter bought it in 1837, increasing its annual production to 200,000 gallons (900,000 liters) and storing the casks in their warehouse beneath Glasgow's Central Station. In 1963 it was bought by Glasgow broker Stanley P. Morrison and today is the flagship distillery of Morrison Bowmore, itself part of the Japanese drinks giant Suntory.

◀ BOWMORE 12-YEAR-OLD
SINGLE MALT: ISLAY 40% ABV
Gently aromatic, with a mix of citrus fruits and smoke on the nose, which carries through to the tongue, together with some dark chocolate.

BOWMORE LEGEND
SINGLE MALT: ISLAY 40% ABV
Dry and bracing, with a faint citrus flavor that develops into a smoky finish.

Bowmore stands on the shores of Loch Indaal. With the salty sea breeze blowing right into the warehouses, some of it is bound to seep into the casks. The distillery has two pairs of stills, six Oregon-pine washbacks, and its own floor maltings, which can supply up to 40 percent of Bowmore's needs. Whether using its own malt, which is peated to around 25 ppm, improves the flavor of Bowmore would be hard to prove, but to see the whole process, from the freshly steeped barley to the peat-fired kiln and its dense blue smoke, certainly makes a visit to the Bowmore Distillery that much more special.

BOWMORE 15-YEAR-OLD ▶
SINGLE MALT: ISLAY 43% ABV
The deep mahogany color comes from two years in Oloroso casks, which also give a raisinlike sweetness to Bowmore's signature note of smoke.

BOWMORE 17-YEAR-OLD
SINGLE MALT: ISLAY 43% ABV
Rich caramel on the nose with a background of peat. Creamy texture, with malt, peat, and fruit interplay on the palate, and a long, warming finish.

Whisky Tour: Islay

The Hebridean island of Islay is the destination for "peat freaks," particularly during the annual malt and music festival, Fèis Ìle, in May. You can either fly to Islay from Glasgow then rent a car to get around, or use the Caledonian MacBrayne ferry from Kennacraig to bring your own vehicle. A four-day itinerary should take in all eight distilleries.

DAY 1: CAOL ILA, BUNNAHABHAIN

1 If arriving in Port Askaig by ferry, the logical place to stay is the charming, family-run Port Askaig Hotel on the coast. From there you can walk to **Caol Ila**, a large Diageo distillery that is the most highly productive on the island.

WASHBACKS AT CAOL ILA

2 It's a car trip or hike along the coastal path from Port Askaig to **Bunnahabhain**, which makes the most lightly peated of the Islay whiskies. It is possible to rent one of the distillery cottages to stay in.

DAY 2: KILCHOMAN, BRUICHLADDICH

3 Tiny **Kilchoman** is Islay's newest and smallest distillery. It's also a farm with a friendly café. Like other Islay distilleries, it sells special bottlings that may not be available elsewhere. This is a great spot for lunch and the dishes use locally sourced ingredients.

4 Drive back over the hill to **Bruichladdich**, which produces a huge array of whiskies. It is near Port Charlotte, where you can learn about illicit whisky production in the Museum of Islay Life, then enjoy dinner at the Port Charlotte Hotel.

BRUICHLADDICH

TOUR STATISTICS

DAYS: 4
LENGTH: 60 miles (96km)
TRAVEL: Car, walking
DISTILLERIES: 8

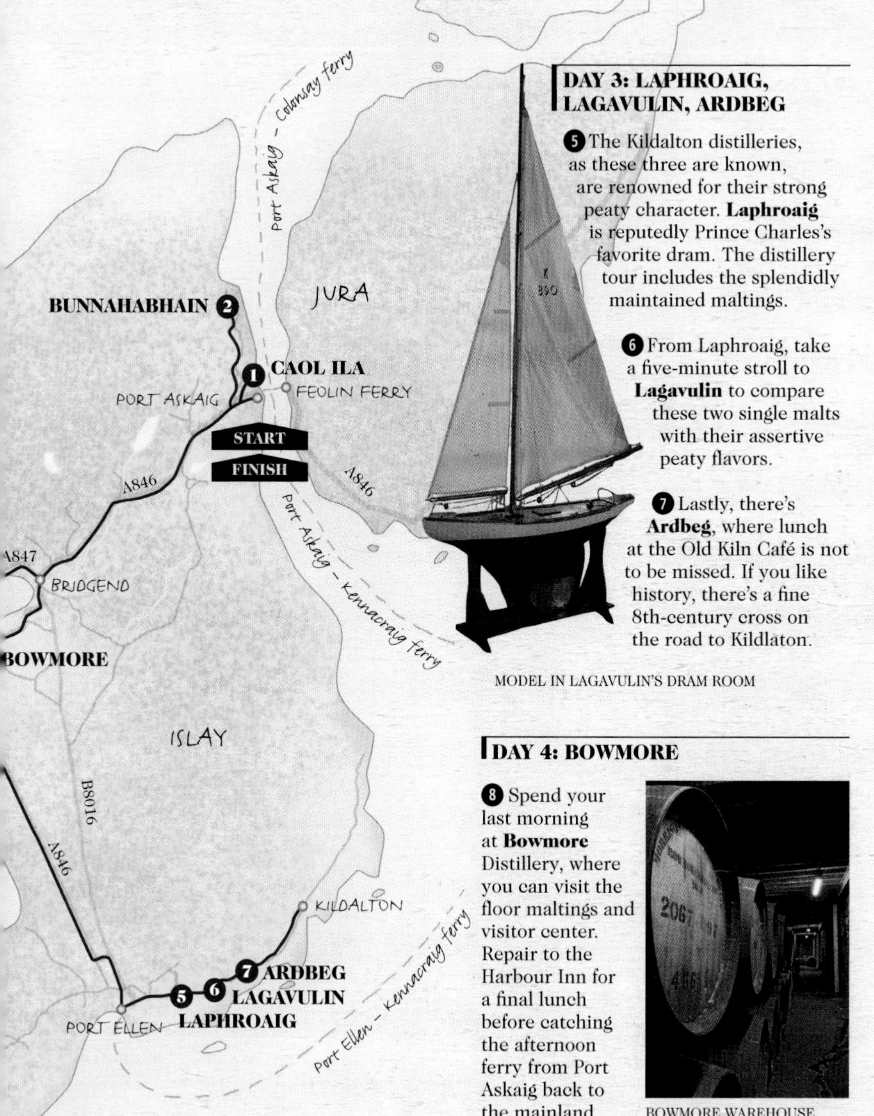

DAY 3: LAPHROAIG, LAGAVULIN, ARDBEG

❺ The Kildalton distilleries, as these three are known, are renowned for their strong peaty character. **Laphroaig** is reputedly Prince Charles's favorite dram. The distillery tour includes the splendidly maintained maltings.

❻ From Laphroaig, take a five-minute stroll to **Lagavulin** to compare these two single malts with their assertive peaty flavors.

❼ Lastly, there's **Ardbeg**, where lunch at the Old Kiln Café is not to be missed. If you like history, there's a fine 8th-century cross on the road to Kildlaton.

MODEL IN LAGAVULIN'S DRAM ROOM

DAY 4: BOWMORE

❽ Spend your last morning at **Bowmore** Distillery, where you can visit the floor maltings and visitor center. Repair to the Harbour Inn for a final lunch before catching the afternoon ferry from Port Askaig back to the mainland.

BOWMORE WAREHOUSE

BRAUNSTEIN

Denmark

Braunstein, Carlsensvej 5, 4600 Koge
www.braunstein.dk

A microbrewery located in an old warehouse in Koge harbor, Braunstein uses a small still to make spirit from malted barley. The resulting spirit is clean, fresh, and fruity. Maturation takes place in ex-Oloroso sherry casks. A new edition of the whiskey is added each year. The distillery also manufactures aquavit, herbal spirits, schnapps, and a beer called BB Amber Lager. Tastings are held each month.

◀ **BRAUNSTEIN**

SINGLE MALT (VARIABLE ABV)

Fruits, raisins, and chocolate come to the fore in this single malt that varies in strength from batch to batch.

BRUICHLADDICH

Scotland
Bruichladdich, Isle of Islay
www.bruichladdich.com

Islay's most westerly distillery stands on the shores of Loch Indaal, across the water from Bowmore. Unlike older distilleries on Islay, it was purpose-built in 1881 with state-of-the-art cavity walls and its own steam generator.

After repeated sales, it was closed it down in 1994, seemingly for good. Then, days before Christmas 2000, it was rescued by a private consortium led by the independent bottler Murray McDavid. From the start, ☛

BRUICHLADDICH 18-YEAR-OLD ▶
SINGLE MALT: ISLAY 46% ABV
There have been two versions of this limited-release bottling: the first finished in German sweet-wine casks, the second in sweet Jurançon casks from France.

BRUICHLADDICH 21-YEAR-OLD
SINGLE MALT: ISLAY 46% ABV
Aged in Oloroso casks and suitably deep in color, this is a pungent, sulfury malt for those who like their whiskies well-sherried.

BRUICHLADDICH

☛ the distiller has been Jim McEwan, who left a long career at Bowmore to join the new venture in 2001.

In 2003 Bruichladdich became the first distillery on Islay to bottle its whiskies on the island. From the heavily sherried Blacker Still and the pink-hued Flirtation, to 3D, Infinity, and The Yellow Submarine, the range of bottlings has been staggering. To date, over 200, many of them in very limited quantities, have been released. While this may cause some frustration among Bruichladdich's devoted fans, it does allow this privately-owned distillery to punch way above its weight.

◄ BRUICHLADDICH WAVES
SINGLE MALT: ISLAY 46% ABV
A multi-vintage vatting that offers a moderately peated style of Bruichladdich.

BRUICHLADDICH PEAT
SINGLE MALT: ISLAY 46% ABV
A powerful phenolic whisky with the scent of bonfires, seaweed, and sweet smoked bacon.

BUCHANAN'S

Scotland
Owner: Diageo

James Buchanan was one of the most notable whisky barons—the Victorian entrepreneurs who brought Scotch to world attention, amassing personal fortunes along the way. Starting as an agent in 1879, he soon began trading on his own and rapidly saw his whisky adopted in the House of Commons. Today the Buchanan's brand is showing signs of prospering once again under its owners, Diageo. Mainly seen in Venezuela, Mexico, Colombia, and the US, Buchanan's is positioned as a premium-style blend. There are two expressions: a 12-year-old and the Special Reserve at 18 years old.

BUCHANAN'S 12-YEAR-OLD ▶
BLEND 40% ABV
Rich on the nose, with sherry and spice. Thinner on the palate, with bitter, dried-lemon notes. Winey, with a touch of dry wood.

BUFFALO TRACE

USA

Buffalo Trace Distillery,
1001 Wilkinson Boulevard,
Frankfort, Kentucky
www.buffalotrace.com

Formerly known as Ancient Age *(see p15)*, Buffalo Trace is located at a crossing point where, in the past, herds of migrating buffalo forded the Kentucky River. The trail they followed was known as the Great Buffalo Trace.

Buffalo Trace boasts the broadest age-range of whiskey in the USA (from 4 to 23 years) and is the only US distillery using five recipes—a wheat whiskey, a rye whiskey, two rye bourbons, and a barley. The Buffalo Trace Experimental Collection of cask strength, wine-barrel-aged whiskeys was launched in 2006.

◀ BUFFALO TRACE KENTUCKY STRAIGHT BOURBON

BOURBON 45% ABV

Aged a minimum of nine years, this has aromas of vanilla, gum, mint, and molasses. Sweet, fruity, and spicy on the palate, with emerging brown sugar and oak. The finish is long, spicy, and fairly dry, with developing vanilla.

BULLEIT

USA
Four Roses Distillery,
1224 Bonds Mill Road,
Lawrenceburg, Kentucky
www.bulleitbourbon.com

Bulleit Bourbon originated in the 1830s with tavern-keeper and small-time distiller Augustus Bulleit, but production ceased after his death in 1860. However, the brand was revived, using the original recipe, in 1987 by his great-great-grandson Tom Bulleit. Seagram subsequently took over the label and from there it passed to Diageo. Bulleit Bourbon is now distilled for Diageo by Four Roses Distillery *(see p124)*, and has a high rye content of 29 percent.

BULLEIT BOURBON ▶
BOURBON 40% ABV
Rich, oaky aromas lead into a mellow flavor, focused around vanilla and honey. The medium-length finish features vanilla and a hint of smoke.

BUNNAHABHAIN

Scotland
Port Askaig, Islay
www.bunnahabhain.com

Before the distilleries found fame for their heavily peat-smoked single malts, their market was not the whisky drinker, but the big blending houses. The blenders only required limited quantities of smoky malt, however, as too much would leave their whiskies unbalanced. With this in mind, Bunnahabhain used unpeated or lightly peated malt.

Bunnahabhain also produces limited-edition bottlings for the Fèis Ìle, Islay's annual festival.

◀ BUNNAHABHAIN 12-YEAR-OLD

SINGLE MALT: ISLAY 40% ABV

A clean, refreshing whisky with a scent of ozone and sea spray, which gives way to a nutty malty sweetness in the mouth.

BUNNAHABHAIN 18-YEAR-OLD

SINGLE MALT: ISLAY 43% ABV

With its richer sherry influence, this has less of the malty distillery character than the 12-year-old. Instead it has a broader texture and woody flavor.

BUSHMILLS

Ireland
2 Distillery Road, Bushmills, County Antrim
www.bushmills.com

Old Bushmills has the amazing ability to be all things to all people: a thoroughly modern distillery housed in a beautiful Victorian building; a boutique distillery that nevertheless produces global brands; and a working distillery that welcomes the public.

Bushmills produces only malt whiskey, so the grain used in its blends is made to order in the Midleton Distillery. This is ☛

BUSHMILLS ORIGINAL ▶
BLEND 40% ABV
A fruity, easy-to-drink, vanilla-infused mouthful. Its clean, clear character makes it very approachable. A lovely entry to the world of Irish whiskey.

BUSHMILLS BLACK BUSH
BLEND 40% ABV
A living legend, Black Bush is the lovable rogue of the family. It is a very classy glassful of honey-nut scrumptiousness with an extremely silky mouthfeel. The benchmark for Irish blends.

BUSHMILLS

matured on site in one of the 10 working warehouses.

Unusually, Old Bushmills doesn't have a problem selling single malts and blends under the same brand name: it is a distillery that isn't afraid to push the boundaries.

◀ BUSHMILLS MALT 10-YEAR-OLD

SINGLE MALT 40% ABV

As you'd expect from a triple-distilled, peat-free whiskey, this charmer appeals to just about everyone. There's a hint of sherry wood, but it is the malt that's showcased here–sweet with hints of fudgy chocolate. A classic and very approachable Irish malt.

BUSHMILLS MALT 16-YEAR-OLD

SINGLE MALT 40% ABV

This malt isn't just a straight aging of the classic 10-year-old. It's a half-and-half mix of bourbon- and sherry-cask-matured malt, married for a further nine months in port pipes. The three woods bring their own magic to bear, and produce a riot of dried-fruit flavors cut with almonds and the ever-present honey.

CAMERON BRIG

Scotland

Cameronbridge Distillery, Winygates, Leven, Fife

Greatly misunderstood, little drunk in their own right, and sadly misrepresented, grain whiskies are Scotch's poor relation. Yet, they are the essential component and base of all blends and, when found as a single grain bottling, the source of much pleasure.

Cameron Brig is made at Diageo's Cameronbridge distillery in Fife, a massive complex of giant continuous stills. The sheer scale of grain whisky production offends some purists but, at its best, good grain whisky is very good indeed. You would not expect anything less from Diageo in its only offering in this category, and Cameron Brig won't disappoint.

CAMERON BRIG 12-YEAR-OLD ▶

SINGLE GRAIN 40% ABV

The nose is clean and grassy, with some honey. Smooth palate; nutty and firm, with a hint of bitter coffee in the finish.

CANADIAN CLUB

Canada

Hiram Walker Distillery,
Riverside Drive East,
Walkerville, Ontario
www.canadianclubwhisky.com

Canadian Club is the oldest and most influential whiskey brand in Canada. Created by businessman Hiram Walker in 1884, it was named simply "Club" and aimed at discerning members of gentlemen's clubs. Unusually, in an era when most whiskeys were sold in bulk, it was supplied in bottles, and thus could not be adulterated by the retailer, a practice soon adopted by other Canadian and American distillers.

◀ CANADIAN CLUB RESERVE
BLEND 40% ABV
Blended at birth, then aged in small oak barrels to give a richer flavor.

CANADIAN CLUB 6-YEAR-OLD 100 PROOF
BLEND 50% ABV
The higher strength allows the signature flavors to come through better with a mixer.

The company has had numerous Royal Warrants, from Queen Victoria to Elizabeth II. A less lofty customer, Al Capone, smuggled thousands of cases across the border during Prohibition.

The Canadian Club brands were sold to Fortune Brands, the owner of Jim Beam *(see p204)*, in 2005. Canadian Club is always "blended at birth"—that is, the component whiskeys are mixed prior to a maturation of at least five years. The standard is a 6-year-old; older versions, such as the 20-year-old, are sometimes released onto the domestic and export markets.

CANADIAN CLUB PREMIUM ▶

BLEND 40% ABV

Creamy and cereal-like; rather spirity. Drier than most Canadian whiskeys, with light smokiness and nuttiness.

CANADIAN CLUB CLASSIC

BLEND 40% ABV

Nose of tropical fruits, oak, and honey, with some toffee. The palate is very smooth and very sweet, with a banana aftertaste.

CANADIAN MIST

Canada

202 MacDonald Road,
Collingwood, Ontario
www.canadianmist.com

Launched in 1965, this whiskey now sells 3 million cases a year in the US. Its distillery is odd in several ways: the equipment is all stainless steel; it is the only Canadian distillery to use a mashbill of corn and malted barley; and it imports its rye spirit from sister distillery Early Times *(see p111)* in Kentucky. Almost all the spirit is tankered to Kentucky for blending. In addition to the popular Canadian Mist brand, the 1185 Special Reserve is also available.

◀ **CANADIAN MIST**

BLEND 40% ABV

Lightly fruity on the nose, with vanilla and caramel notes. Mild, sweet flavor with traces of vanilla toffee.

CAOL ILA

Scotland
Port Askaig, Islay
www.malts.com

For years, Caol Ila played second fiddle to Lagavulin within the Diageo stable. This is beginning to change, as its owners are now promoting Caol Ila as a top-quality single malt.

The distillery was built in 1846, and by 1857 was in the hands of Glasgow blender Bulloch Lade, who reconstructed Caol Ila on a larger scale in 1879.

The distillery was effectively demolished in 1972, re-opening two years later with the warehouse the only part remaining.

CAOL ILA 12-YEAR-OLD ▶
SINGLE MALT: ISLAY 43% ABV
Malty sweetness and citrus aromas balance the scent of tar and peat. Oily textured, with treacly, smoky flavors.

CAOL ILA DISTILLERS EDITION 1995
SINGLE MALT: ISLAY 43% ABV
Sweet, smoky, and malty, with aromatic spices (cinnamon), especially in the lingering finish. The most rounded expression of the core range.

CARDHU

Scotland
Knockando, Aberlour, Morayshire
www.malts.com

Cardhu Distillery was a small farm distillery until Elizabeth Cumming rebuilt it in the 1880s. Soon after, it was sold to Johnnie Walker and became the spiritual home of the blend. In the 1990s, increased demand in Spain for Cardhu 12-year-old led owners Diageo to re-christen the whisky as Cardhu Pure Malt, so they could add other malts and so increase production. But outrage within the industry forced Diageo to withdraw the brand and revert to selling Cardhu as a genuine single malt.

◄ CARDHU 12-YEAR-OLD
SINGLE MALT: SPEYSIDE
40% ABV
A heathery, pear-drop-scented malt. Light to medium body; malty, slightly nutty flavor that finishes fairly short.

CARDHU SPECIAL CASK RESERVE
SINGLE MALT: SPEYSIDE
40% ABV
More depth and body than the 12-year-old, with an aroma of peaches and a sweeter, more creamy texture.

CATDADDY

USA

Piedmont Distillers,
203 East Murphy Street,
Madison, North Carolina
www.catdaddymoonshine.com

Piedmont is the only licensed distillery in North Carolina, and its Catdaddy Moonshine celebrates the state's great heritage of illicit distilling. In 2005, ex-New Yorker Joe Michalek established Piedmont in Madison. It is the first legal distillery in the Carolinas since before Prohibition. "According to the lore of moonshine, only the best moonshine earns the right to be called the Catdaddy," says Joe Michalek. "True to the history of moonshine, every batch of Catdaddy is born in an authentic copper pot still."

CATDADDY CAROLINA MOONSHINE ►

CORN WHISKEY 40% ABV

Triple-distilled from corn in small batches, Catdaddy is sweet and spicy, with notes of vanilla and cinnamon.

CATTO'S

Scotland

Owner: Inver House Distillers

James Catto, an Aberdeen-based whisky blender, set up in business in 1861. His whiskies achieved international distribution on the White Star and P&O shipping lines. After the death of his son Robert in World War I, the company passed to the distillers Gilbey's. More recently, it was acquired by Inver House Distillers. Catto's is a deluxe, fully matured, and complex blend. Two versions are available: a non-age standard bottling and a 12-year-old expression with a yellow-gold, strawlike appearance that belies its complexity and warm finish.

◀ **CATTO'S**

BLEND 40% ABV

The standard Catto blend is aromatic and well-rounded in character, with a smooth, mellow finish.

CHARBAY

USA

Domaine Charbay,
4001 Spring Mountain Road,
St. Helena, California
www.charbay.com

The father-and-son partnership of Miles and Marko Karakasevic are 12th and 13th generation winemakers and distillers. Charbay Double Barrel Hop-Flavored Whiskey is double-distilled in a 1,000-US-gallon (3,750-liter) copper alambic Charentais pot still. It is made using two-row European malted barley, with the addition of hops to the mash for greater aromatic effect. The spirit is put into new American white-oak barrels for maturation.

CHARBAY DOUBLE BARREL ▶
DOUBLE BARREL WHISKEY
64% ABV

The floral nose also features honey, vanilla, oranges, oak, and smoky spice. This big-bodied whiskey offers citrus, spice, and honey on the palate, moving into a long, hoppy, vanilla, and dried-fruit finish.

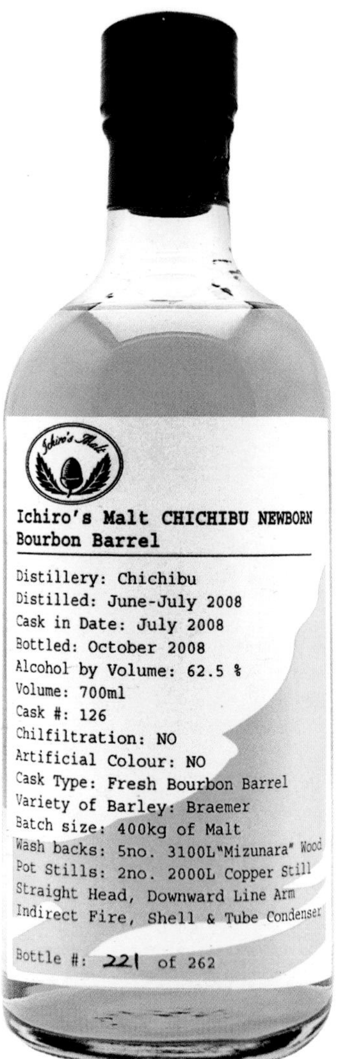

CHICHIBU

Japan

Distribution: Number One Drinks, Netherconesford, King Street, Norwich, UK
www.one-drinks.com

The newest Japanese distillery was founded in 2007 by Ichiro Akuto, previously of Hanyu *(see p175)*. A small plant, it features what might be the only Japanese oak washbacks in the world. Aging takes place in a mix of Japanese oak, ex-bourbon, ex-sherry, and a few ex-cognac casks. Two styles are being tested: one for early maturation; the other for long-term aging. There are plans to malt (or at least kiln) with Japanese peat.

◄ CHICHIBU NEWBORN
NEW MAKE 62.5% ABV
This cannot legally be called whiskey, but gives an idea of the quality to come. Warming, with the typical unripe fruit character of new makes, along with some green pear and jasmine. The palate is clean with well-balanced sweetness.

CHIVAS REGAL

Scotland

Owner: Chivas Brothers

Chivas Brothers was founded in the early 19th century and prospered, due in part to some favorable royal connections. Chivas is owned today by the French Pernod Ricard.

At the heart of Chivas Regal blends are Speyside single malt whiskies, in particular Strathisla Distillery's rich and full single malt. To safeguard the supply of this critically important ingredient, Chivas Brothers bought the distillery in 1950.

CHIVAS REGAL 25-YEAR-OLD ▶

BLEND 40% ABV

The flagship blend, Chivas Regal 25-year-old is classy and rich. A luxury blend for indulgent sipping. Well-mannered, balanced, and stylish.

CHIVAS REGAL 12-YEAR-OLD

BLEND 40% ABV

An aromatic infusion of wild herbs, heather, honey, and orchard fruits. Round and creamy on the palate, with a full, rich taste of honey and ripe apples and notes of vanilla, hazelnut, and butterscotch. Rich and lingering.

CLAN CAMPBELL

Scotland

Owner: Chivas Brothers

Launched as recently as 1984, Clan Campbell is a million-case-selling brand from Chivas Brothers, the whisky arm of drinks giant Pernod Ricard. It is not available in the UK, but is a leader in the important French market, and may also be found in Italy, Spain, and some Asian countries. Despite its relative youth, its origins are now inextricably entwined with Scottish heritage, thanks to clever marketing and a link to the Duke of Argyll, head of the clan. Indeed, what is claimed to be the oldest whisky-distilling relic in Scotland—a distiller's worm—was luckily found on Campbell lands.

◀ **CLAN CAMPBELL**

BLEND 40% ABV

The malt component of Clan Campbell comes largely from Speyside (Aberlour and Glenallachie especially). A smooth, light whisky with a fruity finish.

CLAN MACGREGOR

Scotland
Owner: William Grant & Sons

This budget-priced blend is sold largely in North America and from Venezuela to the Middle East to Thailand, but not by and large in its Scottish homeland. Sales approach an impressive 1.5 million cases a year and it is one of the world's fastest-growing whisky brands. Owned by William Grant & Sons, it is primarily a mix of Grant's own malts (Glenfiddich, Balvenie, and Kininvie) and grain whisky from its substantial Girvan operation. The label proudly carries the badge, motto, and personal crest of the 24th clan chief, Sir Malcolm MacGregor of MacGregor.

CLAN MACGREGOR ▶
BLEND 40% ABV
A blend of grain whiskies and some Speyside malt. Light in style, fragrant, with just a little fruitiness.

THE CLAYMORE

Scotland

Owner: Whyte & Mackay

A claymore is a Highland broadsword. The name was deemed appropriate by DCL (forerunner of drinks giant Diageo) when, in 1977, it attempted to recover some of the market share it had lost when it withdrew Johnnie Walker Red Label from the UK market. Competitively priced, The Claymore was an immediate success. In 1985, the brand was sold to Whyte & Mackay. It continued to sell well for some time, but in recent years has declined and is now principally seen as a low-priced secondary brand. Dalmore is believed to be the main malt whisky in the blend.

◀ **THE CLAYMORE**

BLEND 40% ABV

The nose is heavy and full, with silky mellow tones. Well-balanced and full-bodied on the palate. Polished finish.

CLONTARF

Ireland
www.clontarfwhiskey.com

Clontarf has been in the doldrums for a number of years now, and in that time the taste and style have fluctuated wildly. There isn't a distillery in Clontarf; this is simply a brand, so the whiskeys can come from anywhere. This is a problem, as the consumer loves consistency—especially from blended whiskeys. And with Clontarf you never quite know what you are buying.

CLONTARF SINGLE MALT ▶
SINGLE MALT 40% ABV
Sweet and thin with some nice mouthfeel. Cereal notes with hints of honey, but a bit one-dimensional.

CLONTARF CLASSIC BLEND
BLEND 40% ABV
Toffee popcorn comes to mind when tasting this blend, but not in a good way, unfortunately.

CLUNY

Scotland

Owner: Whyte & Mackay

Although it is produced by Whyte & Mackay, Cluny is supplied in bulk to Heaven Hill Distilleries, which has bottled the whisky in the US since 1988. Today it is one of America's top-selling domestically bottled, blended Scotch whiskies. It contains over 30 malts from all regions of Scotland (Isle of Jura, Dalmore, and Fettercairn single malts among them), along with grain whisky that is almost certainly largely sourced from Whyte & Mackay's Invergordon plant. Cluny is sold primarily on its competitive price. Under Whyte & Mackay's new Indian ownership, it may be a candidate for further international development.

◀ **CLUNY**

BLEND 40% ABV

Subtle sweet and sour nose, with a slight metallic, bitter tang on the palate.

CLYNELISH

Scotland
Brora, Sutherland
www.malts.com

A large, box-shaped distillery dating from 1967, Clynelish has six stills and a capacity of 750,000 gallons (3.4 million liters). Within its grounds is a much older distillery that ran alongside it until 1983. This was Brora, founded in 1819 by the Marquis of Stafford. Known briefly as Old Clynelish, Brora made a heavily peated malt during the 1970s to ensure a supply of Islay-style malts for blends like Johnnie Walker Black Label. In 1983 Brora closed for good, leaving just Clynelish. There have been various rare malts and independent bottlings from Douglas Laing and Cadenhead, among others.

CLYNELISH 14-YEAR-OLD ▶
SINGLE MALT: HIGHLANDS
46% ABV

A mouthfilling malt, quite fruity with a creamy texture, a wisp of smoke, and a firm, dry finish.

COLERAINE

Ireland

Coleraine Distillery Ltd., Hawthorn Office Park, Stockman's Way, Belfast

Never underestimate the selling power of nostalgia: the sole reason this blend is still produced is because whiskey drinkers are very brand loyal, and the name Coleraine still has resonance some three decades after the distillery fell silent. It once produced a single malt of some repute, then in 1954 it started to make grain whiskey for Bushmills, before it was eventually wound down in the 1970s. The reputation of the distillery was such, however, that customers still look out for the name, and so a brand and blend were created to fill a niche. Although the company is called Coleraine Distillery, the whiskey is produced elsewhere.

◄ COLERAINE

BLEND 40% ABV

Light, sweet, and grainy. Probably best suited to drinking with a mixer.

COMPASS BOX

Scotland

www.compassboxwhisky.com

Compass Box was formed in 2000 and describes itself as an "artisanal whisky maker," which may seem disingenuous since it isn't a distiller but a blender, albeit a highly innovative one. Its technique of inserting additional oak staves into a barrel to produce Spice Tree led to pressure from the Scotch Whisky Association and the eventual withdrawal of the product. For all this, the company has been highly influential, and in its short life has won more than 60 medals and awards.

COMPASS BOX THE PEAT MONSTER ▶

BLENDED MALT: ISLAY / SPEYSIDE 46% ABV

Rich and loaded with flavor: a bacon-fat smokiness, full-blown peat, hints of fruit and spice. A long finish, echoing peat and smoke.

COMPASS BOX ASYLA

BLEND 40% ABV

A frequent award-winner. Sweet, delicate, and very smooth on the palate. Flavors of vanilla cream, cereals, and a subtle apple character.

CONNEMARA

Ireland
Cooley Distillery, Riverstown, Cooley, County Louth
www.connemarawhiskey.com

In the eyes of the Irish whiskey industry—and many traditionalists besides—Irish whiskey was a triple-distilled and unpeated drink. Then along came Cooley's John Teeling, who started making Irish whiskey that was double-distilled and peated. It caused quite a stir.

Yet, over the last 15 years, Connemara has gone from being a curiosity to winning gold medals.

◄ CONNEMARA
SINGLE MALT 40% ABV
Definitely its own whiskey rather than "Scotch Light." It is rural, not coastal, so has no iodine or sea spray, just bog heather, fields of barley, and far off peat reek.

CONNEMARA CASK STRENGTH
SINGLE MALT 60.7% ABV
A good splash of water unleashes the nose, which is huge and slightly minty. In the mouth, the beast that had been held in check by the alcohol gets loose and explodes into sparks of dry peat and aromatic timber. The finish is as dry as they come.

CRAGGANMORE

Scotland
Ballindalloch, Morayshire
www.malts.com

This was a well-conceived distillery from the start. Built in 1869, it had a reliable source of pure water from the Craggan burn, nearby access to peat and barley, and its proximity to Ballindalloch station enabled it to become the first distillery in Scotland to have its own railway siding, to bring in supplies and carry off the freshly filled casks. Unusual flat-topped stills and worm tubs may add to Cragganmore's famed complexity.

CRAGGANMORE 12-YEAR-OLD ▶

SINGLE MALT: SPEYSIDE
40% ABV

Floral, heathery aromas, then a robust, woody complexity with a trace of smoke on the palate.

CRAGGANMORE DISTILLERS EDITION 1992

SINGLE MALT: SPEYSIDE
43% ABV

Double-matured, including a spell in a port cask, there is a cherry and orange sweetness that dies away into a lightly smoky finish.

CRAIGELLACHIE

Scotland
Craigellachie, Banffshire

Although the name of John Dewar & Sons is writ large above the modern, plate-glass still house that sits on the main road out of Craigellachie, the distillery was originally tied to White Horse. Peter Mackie, the man behind the famous blend, built Craigellachie in 1891 in partnership with Alexander Edward. Of all the Victorian whisky barons, Mackie was the most connected to malt distilling, having served as an apprentice at Lagavulin, whose whisky was also part of White Horse. Since 1998, Craigellachie has been owned by Bacardi.

◄ CRAIGELLACHIE 14-YEAR-OLD
SINGLE MALT: SPEYSIDE
40% ABV
Rich and aromatic, with a scent of fruit pie and a touch of smoke. More delicate on the tongue, and some woody notes on the finish.

CRAOI NA MONA

Ireland

Cooley Distillery, Riverstown, Cooley, County Louth

Craoi na Móna is Gaelic for "heart of peat." Produced by Cooley, though not one of its own brands, this whiskey can be found in places as diverse as Moscow and London, but so far it hasn't been spotted in Dublin. Given the huge rise in the popularity of Irish whiskey recently, it's not surprising that so many drinks companies are trying to cut themselves a slice of the action. But the market place is very crowded and the amount of whiskey being produced in Ireland is limited. What's left then are too many small companies selling whiskey that's very young indeed.

CRAOI NA MONA ▶
SINGLE MALT 40% ABV
Sweet and young, this is a decidedly immature peated malt.

CRAWFORD'S

Scotland
Owner: Whyte & Mackay / Diageo

Crawford's 3 Star was established by Leith firm A. & A. Crawford, and by the time the company joined the Distillers Company (DCL) in 1944, the blend was a Scottish favorite. Although its popularity continued, it was not of strategic significance to its owners, hence the decision to license the brand to Whyte & Mackay in 1986. Whyte & Mackay are today owned by the Indian UB Group, so the future of this venerable label may lie on the subcontinent. Diageo, successors to DCL, retain the rights to the name Crawford's 3 Star Special Reserve outside the UK. Benrinnes single malt *(see p45)* has been a long-time component in the Crawford's blend.

◀ **CRAWFORD'S 3 STAR SPECIAL RESERVE**
BLEND 40% ABV
A spirity, fruity, fresh-tasting blend, with a smack of citrus, a sweet center, and a dry, slightly sooty finish.

CRESTED TEN

Ireland

Midleton Distillery, Midleton, County Cork

Launched in 1963, Crested Ten was Jameson's first venture into distillery bottling. The fact that it came at least a century after the Scots started branding and distillery bottling shows how far behind the times the Irish industry was and how close it came to vanishing entirely. Crested Ten is a whiskey you'll see lurking on a top shelf in many Irish pubs. It's never on an optic, probably because it's no good with mixers. Instead, you'll have to ask for it by name.

CRESTED TEN ▶
BLEND 40% ABV
An old-fashioned Irish whiskey with plenty of pot-still character and its Oloroso maturation in evidence. This is a great big hug of a drink that will reward those brave enough to take it from the top shelf. Have it neat, cut with just a splash of water.

CROWN ROYAL

Canada

Distillery Road, Gimli, Manitoba
www.crownroyal.ca

Crown Royal was created by Sam Bronfman, President of Seagram, to mark the state visit to Canada of King George VI and Queen Elizabeth in 1939, with its "crown-shaped" bottle and purple velvet bag. Although it was only available in Canada until 1964, it is now one of the best-selling Canadian whiskeys in the US.

Since 1992, it has been produced at the Gimli Distillery on Lake Winnipeg. In 2001, Seagram's shed its alcohol interests and both Gimli Distillery and the Crown Royal brand went to Diageo.

◄ CROWN ROYAL
BLEND 40% ABV
Rich, robust, and balanced. Vanilla, oak, and fruit in the mouthfeel and taste.

CROWN ROYAL SPECIAL RESERVE
BLEND 40% ABV
A big, rich, rounded nose, with fruity (apple, guava, coconut) and floral notes.

CUTTY SARK

Scotland

Owner: Berry Brothers & Rudd

Blended and bottled in Glasgow by The Edrington Group, Cutty Sark was created in 1923 for Berry Bros & Rudd Ltd., a well-established London wine and spirit merchant who is still the brand owner.

The first very pale-colored whisky in the world, Cutty Sark uses some 20 single malt whiskies, many from Speyside distilleries such as Glenrothes and Macallan. The wood for the oak casks is carefully chosen to bring out the characteristic flavor and aroma of each whisky in the Cutty Sark blend and to impart color gently during the long maturation.

CUTTY SARK ORIGINAL ▶

BLEND 40% ABV

Light and fragrant aroma, with hints of vanilla and oak. Sweet and creamy, with a vanilla note, and a crisp finish.

CUTTY SARK 12-YEAR-OLD

BLEND 43% ABV

Elegant and fruity, with a subtle vanilla sweetness. Here the malts used are between 12 and 15 years old.

DAILUAINE

Scotland
Carron, Banffshire
www.malts.com

Under the shadow of Benrinnes, a local farmer called William Mackenzie built Dailuaine in 1854. His son Thomas later went into partnership with James Fleming to form Dailuaine-Talisker Distilleries Ltd. In 1889 Dailuaine was rebuilt and became one of the biggest distilleries in Scotland. The architect Charles Doig erected his first pagoda roof here, to draw smoke from the kiln through the malt. The idea caught on at other distilleries. With all but 2 percent of Dailuaine used as fillings, single malt bottlings are relatively rare.

◄ DAILUAINE GORDON & MACPHAIL 1993
SINGLE MALT: SPEYSIDE
43% ABV
Sweet and malty, with spicy notes of licorice and aniseed. Oaky, toasty notes too. Creamier with a little water.

DALLAS DHU

Scotland
Forres, Morayshire

This late-Victorian distillery, founded in 1898 by the Master Distiller Alexander Edward, was one of many owned by the Distillers Company Limited (DCL) to be shut down in 1983 to await its fate. With just two stills and a waterwheel that had provided the power for the distillery right up until 1971, Dallas Dhu never fully embraced the 20th century. But, while its stills have never been fired up again, it has lived on as a museum run by Historic Scotland. Thousands of visitors have taken the tour and tried a drop of the malt in a blend called Roderick Dhu.

DALLAS DHU RARE MALTS 21-YEAR-OLD ▶
SINGLE MALT: SPEYSIDE
61.9% ABV
Full-bodied, almost Highland character on the nose, with a trace of smoke and a robust, malty flavor.

DALMORE

Scotland
Alness, Ross-shire
www.thedalmore.com

While the Whyte & Mackay blend has a long association with Glasgow, its heart lies in the Highlands, in Dalmore on the banks of the Cromarty Firth. The distillery became part of Whyte & Mackay in 1960, and The Dalmore is now the company's flagship single malt.

The name Dalmore is a fusion of Norse and Gaelic and means "the big meadowland." The distillery stands facing the Black Isle, where some of Scotland's best barley is grown. With ample supplies of

◄ THE DALMORE 12-YEAR-OLD
SINGLE MALT: HIGHLANDS
40% ABV
The well-established 12-year-old has a gentle flavor of candied peel and vanilla fudge.

THE DALMORE 1974
SINGLE MALT: HIGHLANDS
45% ABV
Smooth and full-bodied, with sherry notes, bananas, dark chocolate orange, coffee, walnuts, and a long finish.

grain, plenty of local peat, and water from the Alness River, the site was well-chosen.

For years, the only distillery bottling of Dalmore was a 12-year-old single malt, but in time a 21- and 30-year-old were added, along with Gran Reserva (formerly known as the Cigar Malt) in 2002. That year also saw the sale at auction of a 62-year-old expression for a record-beating £25,877. Since then, the core range has swelled alongside limited-release bottlings. Many of these have played on different cask maturation, a subject that clearly fascinates Whyte & Mackay's Master Blender, Richard Paterson.

THE DALMORE 15-YEAR-OLD ▶
SINGLE MALT: HIGHLANDS
40% ABV

This has the characteristic rich, fruity sherry influence, but with rather more spice—cloves, cinnamon, and ginger.

THE DALMORE 40-YEAR-OLD
SINGLE MALT: HIGHLANDS
40% ABV

After years in American oak casks, this Dalmore was poured into second-fill Matusalem Oloroso sherry butts and then Amoroso sherry wood.

DALWHINNIE

Scotland
Dalwhinnie, Inverness-shire
www.malts.com

Founded in 1897, Dalwhinnie used to claim to be the highest distillery in Scotland, at 1,073 ft (327 m) above sea level, but it has since been eclipsed by Braeval. I ts other claim to fame holds good, however: with a mean annual temperature of just 43°F (6°C), Dalwhinnie remains the coldest distillery in the country. In 1905 it became Scotland's first American-owned distillery, bought by the New York company Cook & Bernheimer, and the Stars and Stripes were raised above the owners' warehouse in Leith. Since 1926 it has been part of DCL (now Diageo), supplying blends such as Black & White.

◄ **DALWHINNIE 15-YEAR-OLD**
SINGLE MALT: HIGHLANDS
43% ABV
Sweet, aromatic, and subtly infused with smoke, this complex malt is thick on the tongue.

DEANSTON

Scotland
Deanston, Perthshire
www.burnstewartdistillers.com

Many distilleries evolved from illicit stills on the farm, others from breweries or malt mills, but only Deanston is a former cotton mill. It was founded in 1785 by Richard Arkwright, one of the great pioneers of the Industrial Revolution. The conversion to whisky-making took place in 1965, in a joint venture with Brodie Hepburn, who also owned Tullibardine. Deanston was soon producing a single malt—Old Bannockburn was released in 1971. Having spent most of the 1980s in mothballs, the distillery was bought by Burn Stewart, now part of Trinidad-based CL Financial, in 1990.

DEANSTON 12-YEAR-OLD ▶
SINGLE MALT: HIGHLANDS
40% ABV

A relatively light-bodied Highland malt, with a nutty flavor and hints of sherry.

DEWAR'S

Scotland
www.dewars.com

When it was bought by Bacardi in 1988, the whole Dewar's enterprise was reinvigorated. The brand was repackaged, with much investment made throughout the business, from distilling to and bottling. New products were developed to augment the standard White Label—one of the biggest selling Scotch blends in the US. First of these was a 12-year-old expression, Special Reserve, followed by the 18-year-old Founder's Reserve bottling, and finally an ultra-premium non-age style known as Signature.

◀ DEWAR'S 12-YEAR-OLD
BLEND 40% ABV
Sweetish and floral. A full and rich blend, with honey and caramel, and licorice notes in the long finish.

DEWAR'S WHITE LABEL
BLEND 40% ABV
Sweet and heathery on the nose. Medium-bodied, fresh, malty, and vaguely spicy, with a clean, slightly dry finish.

The main single malt in the Dewar's blends is Aberfeldy, although the group's other single malts—Aultmore, Craigellachie, Royal Brackla, and MacDuff—are also used.

Dewar's is not widely available in the UK, but is dominant in the US. It is also important in parts of Europe and is gaining a following in Asia. Bacardi has expanded global distribution for Dewar's and greatly expanded its profile through increased advertising and marketing. Standards of production have been kept high, and some would say that the blend quality has improved, especially in the new products.

DEWAR'S 18-YEAR-OLD ▶
BLEND 43% ABV
Here the Dewar's nose is more delicately perfumed, with notes of pear and lemon zest. Soft on the palate, but drying, with a slightly spicy finish.

DEWAR'S SIGNATURE
BLEND 43% ABV
A limited-edition blend, with a heavy share of old Aberfeldy malt. Silky textured and mellow, with rich fruit and dark honey to the fore.

DIMPLE / PINCH

Scotland

Owner: Diageo

Launched to marked success in 1890, Haig's Dimple brand, known as Pinch in the US, is today part of the Diageo stable.

It has always been a deluxe blend, noted for its distinctive packaging introduced by G. O. Haig in the 1890s. It stood out in particular for the wire net over the bottle, originally applied by hand and intended to prevent the cork from popping out in warm climates or during sea transport. It was the first bottle of its type to be registered as a trademark in the United States, although this was done as late as 1958.

◄ DIMPLE 12-YEAR-OLD
BLEND 40% ABV
Aromas of fudge, with woody notes. Hints of mint, and an initial richness on the palate, with candy apples and caramel; spiciness and dried fruits too.

DIMPLE 15-YEAR-OLD
BLEND 43% ABV
In this blend, there are hints of smoke, chocolate, and cocoa, completed by a long, rich finish.

DUFFTOWN

Scotland
Dufftown, Keith, Banffshire
www.malts.com

This epicenter of Speyside whisky-making was bound to have a distillery named after it, although it took until 1896, by which point there were already five distilleries in town. Within a year, Dufftown was owned outright by Peter Mackenzie, who also owned Blair Athol. He was soon selling whisky to the blender Arthur Bell & Sons, who eventually bought Dufftown in 1933. Now part of Diageo, Dufftown continues to supply malt for the Bell's blend and, until recently, had produced little in the way of its own single malt.

SINGLETON OF DUFFTOWN ▶
SINGLE MALT: SPEYSIDE
40% ABV

A sweet and eminently drinkable introductory malt. If this recently launched 12-year-old takes off, there should be plenty available—it comes from one of Diageo's biggest distilleries.

DUNGOURNEY 1964

Ireland

Midleton Distillery, Midleton, County Cork

No one is quite sure how, but for 30 years, some of the last pot still to be produced at the old Midleton Distillery lay undiscovered in the corner of a warehouse at Dungourney. In 1994 the remarkable survivor was bottled and named after the river it had come from some three decades before. Dungourney 1964 is a time machine: one sniff and you are transported back to the days when Jameson, Powers, and Paddy came from competing distilleries.

◄ DUNGOURNEY 1964
IRISH POT STILL WHISKEY
40% ABV

The mushroom edge to the nose gives a hint of age, but the body is still firm. They made whiskey differently back then, which is why this tastes slightly oily, but the tell-tale, almost minty, kick of pure pot still whiskey is still evident.

DYC

Spain

Beam Global España SA, Pasaje Molino del Arco, 40194 Palazuelos de Eresma, Segovia
www.dyc.es

The first whiskey distillery in Spain was founded in 1959 close to Segovia. It stands next to the Eresma River, famous for the excellent quality of its water.

DYC (which stands for Destilerías y Crianza del Whiskey) comes in three versions. The Fine Blend, and the 8-year-old, are both blends of various grains. The Pure Malt is a blended malt. American oak is used for maturation.

DYC 8-YEAR-OLD ▶
BLEND 40% ABV
Floral, spicy, smoky, grassy, with a hint of honey and heather. Smooth, creamy mouthfeel; malty with hints of vanilla, marzipan, apple, and citrus. A bittersweet, long, smooth finish.

DYC PURE MALT
BLENDED MALT 40% ABV
Fragrant bouquet with hints of citrus, sweetness, honey, and vanilla. Full-bodied, rich malt flavor. The finish is long, sophisticated, and subtle, with hints of heather, honey, and fruit.

EAGLE RARE

USA

Buffalo Trace Distillery,
1001 Wilkinson Boulevard,
Frankfort, Kentucky
www.buffalotrace.com

The Eagle Rare brand was introduced in 1975 by Canadian distilling giant Joseph E. Seagram & Sons Inc. In 1989 it was acquired by the Sazerac Company of New Orleans. In its present incarnation, Eagle Rare is part of Sazerac's Buffalo Trace Antique Collection, which is updated annually.

◀ EAGLE RARE 2008 EDITION
BOURBON 45% ABV
This variant of Eagle Rare is from barrels that were distilled in the spring of 1991, and the nose offers caramel, maple syrup, almonds, and vanilla, while the palate boasts more vanilla, worn leather, summer fruits, dark chocolate, and a hint of mint. There is a delicious, spicy, crème brûlée finish.

EARLY TIMES

USA

Brown-Forman Distillery,
850 Dixie Highway,
Louisville, Kentucky
www.brown-forman.com

Early Times takes its name from a settlement near Bardstown where it was created in 1860. It cannot be classified as a bourbon because some spirit is put into used barrels, and bourbon legislation dictates that all spirit of that name must be matured in new barrels.

This version of Early Times was introduced in 1981 to compete with the increasingly popular, lighter-bodied Canadian whiskies. The Early Times mashbill is made up of 79 percent corn, 11 percent rye, and 10 percent malted barley.

EARLY TIMES ▶

KENTUCKY WHISKEY 40% ABV

Quite light on the nose, with nuts and spices. The palate offers more of the same, along with honey and butterscotch notes, leading into a medium-length finish.

EDDU

France

Des Menhirs, Pont Menhir,
29700 Plomelin, Bretagne
www.distillerie.fr

The Des Menhirs Distillery started as a manufacturer of apple cider in 1986, but in 1998 ventured into whiskey. Most fruit distillers that go into whiskey-making use their existing equipment to distill it on the side. Not so Des Menhirs, which built a separate still just for the production of whiskey, which it distills not from barley but from buckwheat (*eddu* in Breton).

◀ EDDU SILVER

BUCKWHEAT WHISKEY
40% ABV

Aromatic rose and heather on the nose. Fruity, with a touch of honey, marmalade, and some nutmeg. Velvety body, with vanilla and oak in the finish.

EDDU GREY ROCK

BLEND 40% ABV

A blended variety containing 30 percent buckwheat. Orange and apricot flavors combine with broom flower. A faint sea breeze is framed by a hint of cinnamon. Balanced flavors and a long, long finish.

EDGEFIELD

USA
2126 Southwest Halsey Street, Troutdale, Oregon
www.mcmenamins.com

Operated by the McMenamin's hotel and pub group, Edgefield Distillery is located in a former dry store for root vegetables on the beautiful Edgefield Manor Estate at Troutdale. The distillery has been in production since February 1998 and features a 12-ft (4-m) tall copper and stainless-steel still. According to McMenamin's, it resembles a hybrid of a 19th-century diving suit and oversized coffee urn, a design made famous by Holstein of Germany, the world's oldest surviving still manufacturer.

EDGEFIELD HOGSHEAD ▶
OREGON WHISKEY 46% ABV
Hogshead whiskey has banana and malt on the sweet, floral nose, with vanilla and caramel notes on the palate, plus barley, honey, and oak in the medium-length finish.

EDRADOUR

Scotland
Pitlochry, Perthshire
www.edradour.co.uk

With an output of just 6,600 gallons (90,000 liters) of pure alcohol a year, this picturesque distillery would have been one of many farm distilleries in the Perthshire hills when it was founded in 1825. Today it feels much more special, and a world apart from the large-scale malt distilleries of Speyside. It became part of Pernod Ricard in 1975 but, as the French group expanded to become a huge global player in the whisky industry, tiny Edradour began to look increasingly out of place. In 2002 it was finally sold to Andrew Symington, owner of independent bottler Signatory.

◀ EDRADOUR 10-YEAR-OLD
SINGLE MALT: HIGHLANDS
40% ABV
Clean peppermint nose, with a trace of smoke. Richer, nutty flavors and a silky texture on the tongue.

ELIJAH CRAIG

USA

Heaven Hill Distillery,
1701 West Breckinridge Street,
Louisville, Kentucky
www.heaven-hill.com

The Reverend Elijah Craig (1743–1808) was a Baptist minister who is widely viewed as the "father of bourbon," having reputedly invented the concept of using charred barrels to store and mature the spirit he made. There seems to be no hard evidence that he was the first person to make bourbon, but the association between a "man of God" and whiskey was seen as a useful tool in the struggle against the temperance movement.

ELIJAH CRAIG 12-YEAR-OLD ▶

BOURBON 47% ABV

A classic bourbon, with aromas of caramel, vanilla, spice, and honey, plus a bit of mint. Full-bodied, rounded on the mellow palate, with caramel, malt, corn, rye, and a little smoke. Sweet oak, licorice, and vanilla dominate the finish.

ELMER T. LEE

USA

Buffalo Trace Distillery,
1001 Wilkinson Boulevard,
Frankfort, Kentucky
www.buffalotrace.com

Elmer T. Lee is a former Master Distiller at Buffalo Trace *(see p66)*, having joined what was then the George T. Stagg Distillery in the 1940s. During his time there, the name changed first to the Albert B. Blanton Distillery (1953), then to the Ancient Age Distillery (1962), and finally to the Buffalo Trace Distillery in 2001. Lee is credited with creating the first modern single barrel bourbon in 1984.

◀ ELMER T. LEE SINGLE BARREL

BOURBON 45% ABV

Aged from six to eight years, this expression offers citrus, vanilla, and corn merging on the fragrant nose, with a full and sweet palate, where honey, lingering caramel, and cocoa notes are also evident.

THE ENGLISH WHISKY CO.

England

St. George's Distillery, Harling Road, Roudham, Norfolk
www.englishwhisky.co.uk

According to Alfred Barnard, in his 1887 tome *Distilleries of the United Kingdom and Ireland,* England had at least four distilleries in the 1800s. These had all gone by the turn of the 20th century and it was not until 2006 that pot stills produced malt spirit in England again, thanks to The English Whisky Co., which hired distilling legend Iain Henderson to set things up.

ENGLISH WHISKY CO. CHAPTER 3 ▶

NEW MAKE 40% ABV

It's not whiskey, as it has not been matured for 3 years, but the new make is very fruity. Iain Henderson also made some peaty spirit in 2007.

EVAN WILLIAMS

USA

Heaven Hill Distillery,
1701 West Breckinridge Street,
Louisville, Kentucky
www.heaven-hill.com

The second biggest-selling bourbon after Jim Beam, Evan Williams takes its name from the person thought by many experts to be Kentucky's first distiller.

Evan Williams was born in Wales but emigrated to Virginia, moving to what would become Kentucky in around 1780. He set up a distillery at the foot of what is now Fifth Street in Louisville.

◀ EVAN WILLIAMS BLACK LABEL

BOURBON 43% ABV

Aromatic, with vanilla and mint notes. The palate is initially sweet, with caramel, malt, and developing leather and spice notes.

EVAN WILLIAMS SINGLE BARREL 1998 VINTAGE

BOURBON 43.3% ABV

Aromatic nose of cereal, dried fruit, caramel, and vanilla. Maple, molasses, cinnamon, nutmeg, and berry notes on the palate. Then a whiff of smoke, plus almonds and honey in the spicy finish.

THE FAMOUS GROUSE

Scotland
Owner: Edrington Group
www.thefamousgrouse.com

The bestselling blend in Scotland was created by the Victorian entrepreneur Matthew Gloag in 1896. At first, it was known simply as The Grouse Brand, but it evolved to become The Famous Grouse. The company was passed down through the generations until 1970, when death duties forced the family to sell out to ☛

THE FAMOUS GROUSE FINEST ▶
BLEND 40% ABV
Oak and sherry on the nose, well balanced with a citrus note. Easygoing, and full of bright Speyside fruit. Clean and medium-dry finish.

THE FAMOUS GROUSE BLENDED MALT RANGE
BLENDED MALTS 43% ABV
Aged at 10-, 12-, 15-, 18-, and 30-years-old, each expression is a blend of malt whiskies from Edrington's distilleries. These are all fruity, spicy whiskies, with vanilla and more tannic, sherry influences becoming increasingly marked through the age range.

THE FAMOUS GROUSE

Highland Distillers, today part of the Edrington Group, which also owns some of Scotland's finest single malt distilleries—Highland Park, Macallan, and Glenrothes among them. Of course, there are high proportions of these whiskies in The Famous Grouse blend.

Since 2007 there has been a number of interesting initiatives. The Black Grouse contains more strongly flavored Islay malt in the blend, while Snow Grouse is a grain whisky, intended to be drunk cold from the freezer, like vodka—a creamy mouth-coating effect results. The Famous Grouse also produces a range of blended malts, aged from 10 to 30 years.

◄ GOLD RESERVE 12-YEAR-OLD

BLEND 40% ABV

Floral and oaky, with a fruity palate, and spicy taste. Rounded off by a long, medium-dry finish.

THE BLACK GROUSE

BLEND 40% ABV

Cream teas, peaches, apples, and jammy aromas. Soft peat and smoke notes on the palate (more so with water), plus vanilla, pepper, and spices, then a gentle finish.

FECKIN IRISH WHISKEY

Ireland
www.feckinwhiskey.com

As Irish whiskey sales continue to buck the trend and sail upward, it's not surprising that bright entrepreneurs continue to pour new products onto the market. From its name to the label, this offering is aimed at the younger end of the spectrum, and there's not a tweed jacket in sight. "Feck," by the way, is a very mild and very Irish swear word that was popularized on the British TV show *Father Ted*.

FECKIN IRISH WHISKEY ▶
BLEND 40% ABV
Made using whiskey from the Cooley Distillery, this is light, approachable, and totally inoffensive. It's clearly a young whiskey and lacks much in the way of depth.

GREAT WHISKEYS

F

FETTERCAIRN

Scotland

Fettercairn, Laurencekirk, Kincardineshire

While the northeastern flank of the Grampians is full of distilleries spilling down to the Spey, the southern slopes are now depleted. Fettercairn stands as their sole survivor. The distillery was established in 1824 as a farm distillery on the Fasque Estate, which was soon bought by Sir John Gladstone, father of the Victorian prime minister William Gladstone. It remained in family hands until 1939, since when it has been bought, sold, and mothballed several times. Today Fettercairn is part of Whyte & Mackay, but their main priorities are in the shape of Dalmore and Jura.

◄ FETTERCAIRN 12-YEAR-OLD
SINGLE MALT: HIGHLANDS
40% ABV

A relatively closed nose gives way to a nutty toffee flavor in the mouth, which dries on the finish.

FORTY CREEK

Canada

Kittling Ridge Distillery,
Grimsby, Ontario
www.fortycreekwhisky.com

Kittling Ridge was named 2008 Canadian Distillery of the Year by *Whisky Magazine*. Unusually, it uses pot stills as well as column stills, and a mashbill of rye, barley, and corn. Built in 1970, it is part of a winery and was originally designed to make *eau de vie*. John Hall, its owner since 1992, brings the skills of a winemaker to distilling: "I am not so bound by tradition as inspired by it." Whiskey critic Michael Jackson called Forty Creek "the most revolutionary whiskey in Canada."

BARREL SELECT ▶
BLEND 40% ABV
A complex, fragrant nose, with soft fruit, honeysuckle, vanilla, and spice. A similar palate, with traces of nuts and leather, and a smooth finish with lingering fruit and vanilla.

FOUR ROSES

USA
1224 Bond Mills Road,
Lawrenceburg, Kentucky
www.fourroses.us

Built to a striking Spanish Mission-style design in 1910, Four Roses Distillery near Lawrenceburg takes its name from the brand first trademarked by Georgia-born Paul Jones, Jr., in 1888. Legend has it that the southern belle with whom he was in love wore a corsage of four red roses to signify her acceptance of his marriage proposal, hence the name he gave to his bourbon.

◀ FOUR ROSES SMALL BATCH
BOURBON 45% ABV
Mild and refined on the nose, with nutmeg and restrained honey. Bold and rich on the well-balanced palate, with spices, fruit, and honey flavors. The finish is long and insinuating, with developing notes of vanilla.

FOUR ROSES SINGLE BARREL
BOURBON (VARIABLE ABV)
A rich, complex nose comprising malt, fruits, spices, and fudge. Long and mellow in the mouth, with vanilla, oak, and a hint of menthol. The finish is long, spicy, and decidedly mellow.

FRYSK HYNDER

The Netherlands
Us Heit distillery, Snekerstraat 43,
8701 XC Bolsward, Friesland
www.usheitdistillery.nl

Us Heit (Frisian for "Our Father") was founded as a brewery in 1970. In 2002, owner Aart van der Linde, a whiskey enthusiast, decided to start distilling whiskey with barley from a local mill. It is the same barley from which Us Heit beer is made and it is malted at the distillery. A 3-year-old single malt, Frysk Hynder, has been released in limited quantities every year since 2005. Us Heit uses different types of cask for maturing, from ex-bourbon barrels to wine casks and sherry butts.

FRYSK HYNDER SHERRY MATURED ▶
SINGLE MALT 43% ABV
Sweetish and remarkably soft for a young whiskey. Tasty, with a beautiful full body and distinct sherry notes.

GEORGE DICKEL

USA

1950 Cascade Hollow Road, Normandy, Tennessee
www.dickel.com

Along with Jack Daniel's, George Dickel is the last licensed, full-scale distillery in Tennessee, though there were around 700 operating there a century ago.

The Dickel operation was moved to Kentucky after Prohibition arrived in Tennessee in 1910, but later returned to a new distillery close to the original location.

◄ GEORGE DICKEL NO. 12

TENNESSEE WHISKEY
45% ABV

Aromatic, with fruit, leather, butterscotch, and a whiff of charcoal and vanilla. Rich palate with rye, chocolate, fruit, and vanilla. The finish offers vanilla toffee and drying oak.

GEORGE DICKEL BARREL SELECT

TENNESSEE WHISKEY 43% ABV

Aromas of corn, honey, nuts, and caramel lead into a full body with soft vanilla, spices, and roast nuts. A long, creamy finish has almond and spices.

GEORGE T. STAGG

USA

Buffalo Trace Distillery,
1001 Wilkinson Boulevard,
Frankfort, Kentucky
www.buffalotrace.com

Part of the Buffalo Trace Antique Collection, George T. Stagg takes its name from the one-time owner of what is now the Buffalo Trace Distillery. In the early 1880s, the distillery was owned by Edmund Haynes Taylor, Jr. During tough economic times, he obtained a loan from his friend Stagg—who later foreclosed on Taylor, taking over his company in the process.

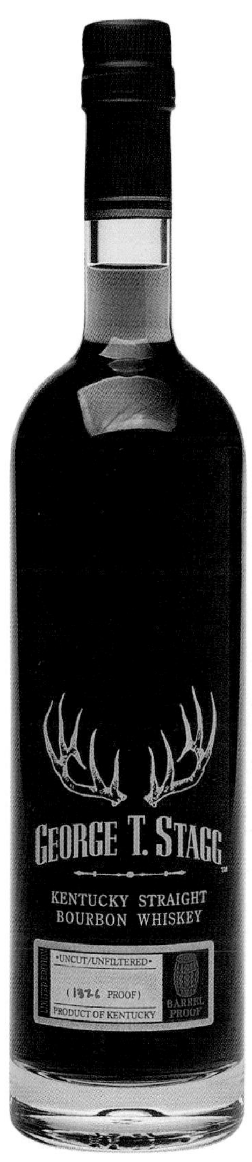

GEORGE T. STAGG 2008 EDITION ▶

BOURBON 72.4% ABV

Distilled in the spring of 1993, this high-strength whiskey boasts a rich nose of butterscotch, marzipan, sweet oak, and cherries. The palate features corn, coffee beans, leather, spice, and oak, with a long toffee and spice finish.

GEORGIA MOON

USA

Heaven Hill Distillery,
1701 West Breckinridge Street,
Louisville, Kentucky
www.heaven-hill.com

Corn whiskey is distilled from a fermented mash of not less than 80 percent corn, and no minimum maturation period is specified. One of the best-known examples is Heaven Hill's Georgia Moon. With a label that promises that the contents be fewer than 30 days old, and available bottled in a mason jar, Georgia Moon harks back to the old days of moonshining.

◀ GEORGIA MOON
CORN WHISKEY 40% ABV
The nose commences with an initial tang of sour liquor, followed by the smell of sweet corn. The palate suggests cabbage water and plums, along with emerging sweeter, candy-corn notes. The finish is short. Drinkers should not expect anything sophisticated.

GIRVAN

Scotland
Aberlour, Banffshire

The distillery at Girvan was established in 1964 by William Grant & Sons in response to a perceived threat to their grain-whisky supplies. Today it includes a grain-whisky distilling complex, a gin distillery, and the recently opened Ailsa Bay single malt distillery. Girvan is rarely bottled by the proprietors as a single grain, but limited numbers of third-party bottlings are occasionally seen. Older expressions are generally dominated by the corn component and are greatly softened by age to provide a delicate and refined whisky of some subtlety and delightful complexity.

GIRVAN 1964 ▶
SINGLE GRAIN 43% ABV
Sweet vanilla nose and a deliciously creamy mouthfeel. Bittersweet caramel palate, with a note of ripe banana.

GLEN BRETON

Canada

Glenora Distillery, Route 19, Glenville, Cape Breton, Nova Scotia
www.glenoradistillery.com

This is North America's only malt whiskey distillery. Cape Breton Island has a strong Scottish heritage, but the Scotch Whisky Association has criticized the name for sounding too much like a Scotch.

Production began in June 1990, halting within weeks due to lack of funds. The distillery was later bought by Lauchie MacLean, who has re-distilled earlier, inconsistent spirit, and bottles at 8 or 9 years.

Glenora has its own maltings and uses Scottish barley that is given a light peating. The two stills it uses are made by Forsyths of Rothes.

◄ **GLEN BRETON RARE**
SINGLE MALT 43% ABV
A butterscotch, heather, ground ginger, and honey nose. Light to medium body, with a creamy mouthfeel and notes of wood, almonds, caramel, and peat.

GLEN DEVERON

Scotland

Macduff Distillery, Banff, Aberdeenshire

While the single malt is Glen Deveron (named after the water source—the Deveron River in eastern Speyside), the distillery is called Macduff. It was founded in 1962 by a consortium led by the Duff family. Much of the malt was used in blends, particularly William Lawson, whose owners bought the distillery in 1972. Since then it has changed hands twice, increased its number of stills to five, and now belongs to Bacardi. Various age statements are produced, and, just to confuse matters, there are occasional independent bottlings under the name Macduff.

GLEN DEVERON 10-YEAR-OLD ▶

SINGLE MALT: HIGHLANDS 40% ABV

Although it is described as a "Pure Highland Single Malt" on the bottle's label, in style this is a classic, clean, gentle Speyside whisky.

GLEN ELGIN

Scotland
Longmorn, Morayshire
www.malts.com

The Glen Elgin distillery was founded in 1898, when demand for Speyside malt from the blenders was at its peak.

But boom soon turned to bust, the industry entered a long slump, and production at Glen Elgin was intermittent during its first three decades, as the business passed from one owner to the next.

After many years of appearing only in blends (notably White Horse), a first distillery bottling of Glen Elgin was released in 1977.

◀ GLEN ELGIN 12-YEAR-OLD
SINGLE MALT: SPEYSIDE
43% ABV
This is one of the most floral and perfumed Speyside malts, with a nutty, honey-blossom aroma and a balanced flavor that goes from sweet to dry.

GLEN ELGIN 16-YEAR-OLD
SINGLE MALT: SPEYSIDE
58.5% ABV
The 16-year-old is a non chill-filtered, cask-strength malt with a deep mahogany color and a ripe, fruitcake flavor from its years in European oak.

GLEN GARIOCH

Scotland
Oldmeldrum, Inverurie, Aberdeenshire
www.glengarioch.com

This small Aberdeenshire distillery was founded in 1798, yet the first distillery bottling of Glen Garioch as a single malt was not until 1972. It survived the long years in between thanks to its popularity among blenders.

Glen Garioch is now part of Morrison Bowmore, which bottles most, if not all of, the distillery's limited production as a single malt in a range of age statements, from 8 to 21 years old.

GLEN GARIOCH 15-YEAR-OLD ▶
SINGLE MALT: HIGHLANDS
43% ABV
A floral, heathery nose offers notes of Lapsang tea. On the palate it has a malty flavor that dries to a spicy finish.

GLEN GARIOCH 21-YEAR-OLD
SINGLE MALT: HIGHLANDS
43% ABV
A smooth, well-rounded malt with a luscious syrupy texture and a mellow, ripe fruit character that shows some influence from sherry casks.

GLEN GRANT

Scotland
Rothes, Morayshire
www.glengrant.com

Glen Grant, built in 1840, was the first of the five distilleries in the town of Rothes.

It was a very good site for a distillery, with the Glen Grant burn supplying water for the mash and to power the machinery, and plentiful supplies of grain from the barley fields of nearby Moray.

Having been with Pernod Ricard from 2001–2006, it is now with the Italian Campari group. Though it receives little attention at home, it is one of the top five bestselling malts in the world.

◄ GLEN GRANT SINGLE MALT
SINGLE MALT: SPEYSIDE
40% ABV
Light, spirity, and floral on the nose. Initially dry on the palate, but softer, nut flavors develop. A herby finish rounds off this aperitif-style whisky.

GLEN GRANT 10-YEAR-OLD
SINGLE MALT: SPEYSIDE
40% ABV
A relatively dry nose with the scent of orchard fruit. Light to medium body with a cereal, nutty flavor.

GLEN KEITH

Scotland
Keith, Banffshire

Having bought Strathisla in 1950, Seagram built Glen Keith on the site of an old grain mill seven years later. Both are in Keith and were part of Seagram's whisky arm, Chivas Brothers (now part of Pernod Ricard). Both also shared a simple function—to supply the company's bestselling brands. Glen Keith began life using triple distillation and later pioneered the use of computers in its whisky-making at a time when some distilleries had only recently joined the national power grid.

Glen Keith was mothballed in 2000 and, while independent bottlings are available, its 10-year-old is increasingly hard to find.

GLEN KEITH 10-YEAR-OLD ►
SINGLE MALT: SPEYSIDE
43% ABV
This relatively rare official bottling is a mix of grassy Speyside aromas and some toffee sweetness on the tongue.

GLEN ORD

Scotland

Muir of Ord, Ross-shire
www.malts.com

Despite its name, Glen Ord is not in a valley, but on the fertile flatlands of the Black Isle, north of Inverness. It was founded in 1838, close to the alleged site of the Ferintosh Distillery, which was established in the 1670s. In 1923 Glen Ord was bought by John Dewar & Sons, shortly before they joined the Distillers Company Limited (DCL).

With six stills and 750,000 gallons (3.4 million liters) of production, it has plenty to spare for a single malt. This has been called Ord, Glenordie, and Muir of Ord at various times. Recent bottlings are called The Singleton of Ord, aiming at the US market.

◀ GLEN ORD 12-YEAR-OLD
SINGLE MALT: HIGHLANDS
43% ABV

This citrusy, orange-peel-scented malt has a gentle apple-pie flavor and some spicy ginger notes on the finish.

GLEN SCOTIA

Scotland
Campbeltown, Argyll
www.lochlomonddistillery.com

Strung-out at the far end of the Mull of Kintyre, Campbeltown's rise and fall as "whiskyopolis" has been well-documented, as has the story of the Springbank Distillery, which managed to pull through and now enjoys cult status *(see p321)*. But, it was not the only one, for the much lesser known Glen Scotia also survived. With its single pair of stills, Campbeltown's "other" distillery was founded in the 1830s by the Galbraith family, who retained control for the rest of the century. After various owners followed, it was bought by Glen Catrine (Loch Lomond Distillers) in 1994.

GLEN SCOTIA 12-YEAR-OLD ▶
SINGLE MALT: CAMPBELTOWN
40% ABV
This distillery bottling replaced the 8-year-old and has a spicy aroma with sweeter, richer notes on the palate.

GLEN SPEY

Scotland

Rothes, Aberlour, Banffshire
www.malts.com

James Stuart was an established distiller with Macallan and the key partner in building the Glenrothes Distillery in 1878, although he quickly pulled out of that venture. A few years later, he decided to convert an oat mill he owned into Glen Spey, on the opposite bank of the Rothes burn from Glenrothes. The project inevitably led to disputes over water rights. In 1887, Glen Spey was sold to the London-based gin distiller Gilbey's, who later merged with Justerini & Brooks. Its J&B blend has contained Glen Spey ever since. The current owners, Diageo, have just one malt bottling in their Flora & Fauna range.

◀ GLEN SPEY FLORA & FAUNA 12-YEAR-OLD

SINGLE MALT: SPEYSIDE
43% ABV

A light, grassy nose and brisk, nutty flavor. Very dry, with a short finish.

GLENALLACHIE

Scotland
Aberlour, Banffshire

This modern gravity-flow distillery was established by a subsidiary of the giant Scottish & Newcastle Breweries in 1967. The architect was William Delmé-Evans, who had earlier designed and part-owned Tullibardine and Jura. With the capacity to produce 615,000 gallons (2.8 million liters) of pure alcohol a year, there should be plenty available for a single malt. And yet, so far there have only been a few independent bottlings and a 16-year-old cask strength expression from the distillery's current owners, Chivas Brothers (Pernod Ricard).

GLENALLACHIE 16-YEAR-OLD 1990 ▶
SINGLE MALT: SPEYSIDE
56.9% ABV
A dark, heavily sherried whisky matured in first-fill Oloroso casks, which can be hard to find.

GLENBURGIE

Scotland
Glenburgie, Forres, Morayshire

Glenburgie began life as the Kilnflat Distillery in 1829. It was renamed Glenburgie in 1878 and, after various changes in ownership, became part of Canada's Hiram Walker in the 1930s. From then on, the primary role of this distillery was to supply whisky for Ballantine's Finest. Yet, as early as 1958, long before most of Speyside began thinking of single malt, Glenburgie released its own bottling under the name Glencraig. In 2004, its then owners, Allied Distillers, demonstrated their faith in Glenburgie by investing £4.3m. The distillery was completely rebuilt and only the stills and milling equipment were kept.

◀ GLENBURGIE 15-YEAR-OLD
SINGLE MALT: SPEYSIDE
46% ABV
On the fruitier side of Speyside, with a relatively luscious texture and notes of stewed plums.

GLENCADAM

Scotland

Brechin, Angus
www.glencadamdistillery.co.uk

With the demise of Lochside in 2005, Glencadam became the only distillery left in Angus. It was founded in 1825 by George Cooper and, despite various changes in ownership, remained in private hands until 1954, when it became part of Hiram Walker and later Allied Distillers. While there was some safety in numbers on Speyside, Glencadam looked increasingly isolated. When it shut down in 2000—a victim of overproduction in the industry—its prospects looked bleak. But it slipped back into independent hands in 2003 when bought by Angus Dundee *(see p17)*.

GLENCADAM 10-YEAR-OLD ▶
SINGLE MALT: HIGHLANDS
46% ABV

The nose is fresh and grassy, with citrus notes and a trace of spicy oak. Rounded on the palate, citrusy and crisp. Well-balanced, with a long finish.

GLENDRONACH

Scotland

Forgue, Huntly, Aberdeenshire

This distillery is the spiritual sister to Ardmore, and fellow contributor to the Teacher's blend. Although William Teacher & Sons did not buy Glendronach until 1960, the firm had sourced Glendronach malts for years. After Teacher's was swallowed up by Allied Distillers, Glendronach was picked, in 1991, to be one of the "Caledonian Malts"—the company's belated riposte to UDV's Classic Malts. A decade later, after five years in mothballs, the distillery re-opened. By that time the single malts had become less peaty and were matured in American oak ex-bourbon casks rather than sherry casks.

◄ **GLENDRONACH 12-YEAR-OLD**

SINGLE MALT: SPEYSIDE
40% ABV

This dense, heavily sherried malt replaced the 15-year-old and is best suited to after-dinner sipping.

GLENDULLAN

Scotland
Dufftown, Keith, Banffshire
www.malts.com

There were already six distilleries in Dufftown when the Aberdeen-based blenders William Williams & Sons decided to build a seventh. Work on Glendullan began in 1897, and within five years, its whisky had secured a royal warrant from the new king, Edward VII. It has been in almost continual production ever since, and for years was a key filling in the deluxe Old Parr blend *(see p277)*. In the 1960s, a modern distillery was erected next door, and for the following 20 years the two sides of Glendullan worked in tandem. Today, the modern distillery carries on alone.

GLENDULLAN FLORA & FAUNA 12-YEAR-OLD ▶
SINGLE MALT: SPEYSIDE
43% ABV
A crisp, aperitif-style malt with a sweeter palate than you would expect.

GLENFARCLAS

Scotland
Ballindalloch, Banffshire
www.glenfarclas.co.uk

The oldest family-owned distillery in Scotland has belonged to the Grants since 1865, when John Grant and his son George took over the tenancy of Rechlarich farm, near Ballindalloch. It gradually assumed importance in the family business, and went on to become the Glenfarclas-Glenlivet Distillery Company in partnership with the Pattison Brothers of Leith, whose bankruptcy at the end of the 19th century almost dragged the Glenfarclas distillery down with it.

◄ GLENFARCLAS 105
SINGLE MALT: SPEYSIDE
60% ABV
A cask strength 10-year-old. Water dampens the fiery edge and brings out a sweet, nutty-spicy character.

GLENFARCLAS 10-YEAR-OLD
SINGLE MALT: SPEYSIDE
40% ABV
This rich, malty whisky with a smoky, aromatic nose is a nod to the Highlands.

Surrounded by 10 large dunnage warehouses, Glenfarclas is no boutique distillery. It boasts a modern mill and six stills. It also claims to be the first malt distillery to have offered a cask strength expression—Glenfarclas 105 was released in 1968. At the time, the industry doubted that single malts, let alone something that was 60 percent pure alcohol, would catch on with the whisky buyer.

Recently, Glenfarclas offered 10 vintage expressions, ranging from 1952 to 1989. The house style is a robust, outdoors take on Speyside, with a greater affiliation to sherry butts than bourbon barrels.

GLENFARCLAS 12-YEAR-OLD ▶
SINGLE MALT: SPEYSIDE
43% ABV

A distinct sherry nose, with spicy flavors of cinnamon and stewed fruit.

GLENFARCLAS 15-YEAR-OLD
SINGLE MALT: SPEYSIDE
46% ABV

Described by writer Dave Broom as "George Melly in a glass," for its fruity, over-the-top exuberance. It is intensely perfumed, sherried, and powerful.

GLENFIDDICH

Scotland
Dufftown, Keith, Banffshire
www.glenfiddich.com

With a wife and nine children to support on a salary of £100 a year, William Grant had to scrimp and save until he raised the funds to start Glenfiddich in 1886. Using stones from the bed of the Fiddich River, and second-hand stills from neighboring Cardhu, he was able to produce his first spirit on Christmas Day 1887. From these humble beginnings, Glenfiddich has grown into the biggest malt distillery in the world. By the time William Grant died in 1923, his

◀ GLENFIDDICH 12-YEAR-OLD
SINGLE MALT: SPEYSIDE
40% ABV

A gentle aperitif-style whisky with a malty, grassy flavor and a little vanilla sweetness. Quite soft.

GLENFIDDICH 15-YEAR-OLD SOLERA RESERVE
SINGLE MALT: SPEYSIDE
40% ABV

After 15 years in American oak, this is finished off in Spanish casks for an extra-soft layer of fresh fruit and spice.

firm was already producing its own blends, which were sold as far afield as Australia and Canada. The company also pioneered today's market for single malts in the 1960s—there was no big brand before Glenfiddich.

Today Glenfiddich has 29 stills and a capacity of 2.2 million gallons (10 million liters) of pure alcohol a year. In time this will be matched by Diageo's new Roseisle Distillery, but it is believed that Roseisle will supply malt for the likes of Johnnie Walker. For the moment, Glenfiddich's pole position as the most popular malt whisky in the world looks secure.

GLENFIDDICH 18-YEAR-OLD SOLERA RESERVE ▶

SINGLE MALT: SPEYSIDE
40% ABV

A big step up from the 12-year-old: ripe tropical fruit flavors, a pleasant oaky sweetness, and a trace of sherry.

GLENFIDDICH 21-YEAR-OLD CARIBBEAN RUM CASK

SINGLE MALT: SPEYSIDE
40% ABV

Rich, toffee-flavored malt with flavors of bananas, caramel, spice, and chocolate orange.

Whisky Tour: Speyside

Speyside boasts the greatest concentration of distilleries in the world. Distillery tours were pioneered here, when William Grant & Sons first opened Glenfiddich to the public in 1969. Its competitors laughed—but soon opened their own centers. Speyside hosts two whisky festivals each year, in May and September. Convenient accommodation options include the Highlander Inn in Craigellachie and The Mash Tun in Aberlour.

DAY 1: GLENFIDDICH, THE BALVENIE

❶ Begin at Dufftown's **Glenfiddich**, the ultimate home of whisky tourism. The distillery offers a free tour or an extended option with tastings at extra cost. You need to pre-book for the extended tour, which lasts two and a half hours.

❷ After lunch at Glenfiddich, take in sister distillery **The Balvenie**. The three-hour guided tour here, which must also be pre-booked, includes the floor maltings and tastings of exclusive vintages.

THE BALVENIE

DAY 2: COOPERAGE, ABERLOUR, THE MACALLAN, CARDHU

❸ Head to Craigellachie to start the day at the **Speyside Cooperage**. There you can watch a film about cask-making and see the coopers at work from a viewing gallery.

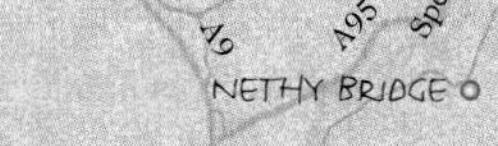

ABERLOUR CASKS

❹ Afterward, take the A95 toward **Aberlour** Distillery, which is the next stop. Again, pre-booking is advisable. The tour culminates in a tasting and the chance to bottle your own whisky from the cask.

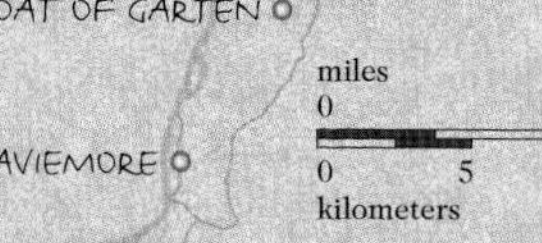

5 Head over the Spey, pausing to admire the Thomas Telford bridge (built in 1812), then take the B9102 to **The Macallan**. Its "Precious Tour" is the one to pre-book for its tutored nosing and tasting of a range of Macallan whiskies.

6 **Cardhu** Distillery is further along the B9102, which you can visit without pre-booking. The malt made here is used in the Johnnie Walker blends.

DAY 3: GRANTOWN-ON-SPEY, THE WHISKY CASTLE, THE GLENLIVET, GORDON & MACPHAIL

7 **Grantown-on-Spey** is the gateway to the Cairngorms National Park. It's a handy place to pick up provisions, and has a good little whisky shop on the High Street called the Wee Spey Dram.

8 Head east from Grantown to get to Tomintoul, where **The Whisky Castle** shop has an excellent selection of Scotch malts.

9 Pre-register on **The Glenlivet** website *(www.theglenlivet.com)* as a "Guardian" to gain access to a secret room where you can enjoy some unusual drams. The free tour is a good introduction to the oldest legal distillery on Speyside; better still is its three-day Whisky School.

10 The final stop is a place of pilgrimage for serious whisky fans: the **Gordon & MacPhail** shop in Elgin. Here you'll find all your favorites, some rare bottles, and exceptional value in G&M's own bottlings from their vast stock of whiskies.

TOUR STATISTICS

DAYS: 3
LENGTH: 90 miles (145km)
TRAVEL: Car, or bus and taxi
DISTILLERIES: 8

GORDON & MACPHAIL

GLENGOYNE

Scotland

Drumgoyne, Stirlingshire
www.glengoyne.com

The Campsie Fells were once a hotbed of whisky smuggling. Before the Excise Act of 1823, there were at least 18 illicit distillers in this corner of Stirlingshire. Among them was probably George Connell, who finally took out a license for his Burnfoot Distillery in 1833. It went on to become Glenguin and eventually Glengoyne in 1905.

◄ GLENGOYNE 10-YEAR-OLD
SINGLE MALT: HIGHLANDS
40% ABV

This unpeated whisky has a clean, grassy aroma, with a nutty sweetness that comes through on the palate.

GLENGOYNE 12-YEAR-OLD CASK STRENGTH
SINGLE MALT: HIGHLANDS
57.2% ABV

Non chill-filtered and bottled at cask strength, this 12-year-old is the purest representation of the distillery. Lightly sweet nose, with notes of heather, pear drops, and marzipan. Malty, cereal palate, seasoned with black pepper.

By then the distillery was owned by the blending house of Lang Brothers, who were bought out in the 1960s by Robertson & Baxter, now the Edrington Group. In 2001 it released a novel expression of Glengoyne, involving the first ever use of Scottish oak casks. Two years later, the distillery was sold to the blender and bottler Ian MacLeod & Co. The number of single malts has grown dramatically and includes single cask bottlings alongside the core range.

GLENGOYNE 21-YEAR-OLD ▶
SINGLE MALT: HIGHLANDS
43% ABV

Now matured entirely in first-fill sherry casks, this is a rich, after-dinner malt, with notes of brandy butter, cinnamon, and sweet spice.

GLENGOYNE 17-YEAR-OLD
SINGLE MALT: HIGHLANDS
43% ABV

This whisky has a rich, sherried nose with butterscotch and molasses flavors, with some citrus notes.

GLENKINCHIE

Scotland
Pencaitland, Tranent, East Lothian
www.malts.com

Robert Burns described the rolling farmland south of Edinburgh as "the most glorious corn country I have ever seen," and it was here at Pencaitland that John and George Rate founded Glenkinchie in 1825.

In more recent history, the Glenkinchie 10-year-old was picked as one of the original Classic Malts by Diageo in 1988. New expressions have recently been added, and the 10 has been replaced with a 12-year-old.

◄ GLENKINCHIE 12-YEAR-OLD
SINGLE MALT: LOWLANDS
43% ABV
The nose reveals a sweet, grassy aroma with a faint wisp of smoke. In the mouth it has a firm, cereal flavor and a touch of spice at the end.

GLENKINCHIE 20-YEAR-OLD
SINGLE MALT: LOWLANDS
58.4% ABV
Aged in bourbon casks and then re-racked into brandy barrels, the 20-year-old has a luscious, mouth-coating texture and plenty of spicy, stewed fruit flavors.

GLENLIVET

Scotland
Ballindalloch, Banffshire
www.theglenlivet.com

In the early 19th century, Glen Livet was a glen dedicated to making moonshine after the harvest—there were at least 200 illicit stills in this small corner of Speyside. Among them was George Smith, who in 1824 established Glenlivet as a licensed distillery. But breaking ranks with the smuggling fraternity meant that Smith had to carry revolvers for his protection.

Smith began supplying Andrew Usher in Edinburgh who ☛

THE GLENLIVET 12-YEAR-OLD ▶
SINGLE MALT: SPEYSIDE
40% ABV
Citrusy and heathery, with a scent of fresh wood and soft fruit, a light to medium body, and a dry, clean finish.

THE GLENLIVET FRENCH OAK RESERVE 15-YEAR-OLD
SINGLE MALT: SPEYSIDE
40% ABV
A smoother, richer take on the 12-year-old, with a malty, strawberries-and-cream flavor laced with spice.

GLENLIVET

☛ bottled a prototype blend, Old Vatted Glenlivet, in 1853. As blended Scotch took off, demand for "Glenlivet-style" malts to feed the blends soared. Distillers all down the Spey bolted the magic name "Glenlivet" to their distillery and hoped the blenders would beat a path to their door.

Glenlivet's current owner—the French giant Pernod Ricard—seems eager to seize poll position among top-selling malts. In 2008 it announced plans to boost capacity to 2.2 million gallons (10 million liters), the same as Glenfiddich.

◀ THE GLENLIVET XXV

SINGLE MALT: SPEYSIDE
43% ABV

This 25-year-old is a sumptuous after-dinner malt of real complexity, with flavors of candied orange peel and raisins, and an intense nutty, spicy character.

THE GLENLIVET 18-YEAR-OLD

SINGLE MALT: SPEYSIDE
43% ABV

This whisky has far more depth and character than the standard 12-year-old. Honeyed, fragrant, and dries to a long, nutty finish.

GLENLOSSIE

Scotland
Elgin, Morayshire
www.malts.com

Glenlossie was built in 1876 by John Duff, the former manager of Glendronach. For a century it was a single entity, and part of DCL from 1919. Its role was simply to pump out malt whisky for blends. Yet, within the industry, the quality of Glenlossie was appreciated and it was one of only a dozen to be designated “top class.” It now shares its site with Mannochmore, a new distillery built in 1971.

Glenlossie has produced a 10-year-old since 1990, although there have been a fair number of independent bottlings from Gordon & MacPhail, among others.

GLENLOSSIE FLORA & FAUNA 10-YEAR-OLD ▶
SINGLE MALT: SPEYSIDE
43% ABV
Grassy and heathery, with a smooth, mouth-coating texture and a long spicy finish.

GLENMORANGIE

Scotland
Tain, Ross-shire
www.glenmorangie.com

Glenmorangie started life as an old farm distillery, but was licensed in 1843 by William Matheson, who was already involved with Balblair. It remained a rustic operation for years. In the 1880s Alfred Barnard described Glenmorangie as "the most ancient and primitive we have seen" and "almost in ruins."

Outside investors were brought in just in time and the distillery was rebuilt. For much of the 20th century, its key role was to supply malt for blends such as Highland Queen and James Martin's. In

◄ **GLENMORANGIE ORIGINAL**
SINGLE MALT: HIGHLANDS
40% ABV
This is the ever-popular 10-year-old. It has honeyed flavors with a hint of almonds.

GLENMORANGIE 18-YEAR-OLD
SINGLE MALT: HIGHLANDS
43% ABV
A rich, well-rounded whisky, with dried fruit notes and a distinctive nuttiness from its finishing in sherry butts.

the 1970s, though, Glenmorangie started laying down casks for a 10-year-old single malt. It was the best decision the company ever made—by the late 1990s, this had become the best-selling single malt in Scotland.

Glenmorangie's stills are tall and thin, and produce a light, very pure spirit. The real skill of the distillery has been in the way it has combined this elegant spirit with wood—indeed, Glenmorangie has been a pioneer of wood finishes. After endless experiments with increasingly exotic barrels, it is an expert in how a particular cask can twist and refocus a mature malt before bottling.

GLENMORANGIE 25-YEAR-OLD ▶

SINGLE MALT: HIGHLANDS
43% ABV

Packed with flavor, this produces dried fruit, berries, chocolate, and spice. An intense and complex whisky.

GLENMORANGIE NECTAR D'OR

SINGLE MALT: HIGHLANDS
46% ABV

Here, the Glenmorangie honeyed floral character is given a twist of spice and lemon tart from Sauternes casks.

GLENROTHES

Scotland
Rothes, Morayshire
www.glenrotheswhisky.com

After Dufftown, Rothes is the second busiest whisky town on Speyside. Not that you would know it: the distilleries are tucked discreetly out of sight, including Glenrothes, which sits quietly in a dip beside the Rothes burn.

After its founding in 1878, Glenrothes began to build a reputation among blenders for the quality of its malt. It seemed as if there was never any to spare—until 1987, when the first single

◄ THE GLENROTHES 1994
SINGLE MALT: SPEYSIDE
43% ABV
A satisfyingly complex malt with a fruity, toffee-scented bouquet that leads to a soft citrus flavor and long, gentle finish.

THE GLENROTHES 1978
SINGLE MALT: SPEYSIDE
43% ABV
A very rare expression, released in 2008, with a concentrated plum pudding and molasses character, a silky, honeyed texture and great length.

malt, a 12-year-old was released. At first, Glenrothes failed to stand out: it had entered the 12-year-old stakes late in the day and there was plenty of competition, particularly on Speyside.

This all changed with the launch of the highly acclaimed Glenrothes Vintage malt in 1994. The brand owners, wine merchants Berry Brothers & Rudd, realized vintage variation might be appreciated by malt-whisky-lovers as well as wine-lovers. In 2004, Glenrothes Select Reserve was released to provide continuity between vintages.

THE GLENROTHES SELECT RESERVE ▶

SINGLE MALT: SPEYSIDE
43% ABV

Like non-vintage Champagne, this is a vatting of different ages to produce a complex whisky with notes of hard candy, ripe fruit, vanilla, and spice. Sweeter on the nose than in the mouth.

THE GLENROTHES 1975

SINGLE MALT: SPEYSIDE
43% ABV

Increasingly hard to find, this vintage offers big, rich flavors—stewed fruits, toffee, bitter chocolate, and orange peel. Medium-sweet satisfying finish.

GLENTAUCHERS

Scotland

Mulben, Keith, Banffshire

Many late-Victorian distilleries sprang up in the hope of finding a market among whisky blenders but, in 1897, Glentauchers was built explicitly to supply Buchanan's blend, which evolved into the top-selling Black & White. The distillery was a joint venture between James Buchanan and the Glasgow-based blender W. P. Lowrie. They chose an ideal site, right by a main road that connected to the east-coast train line from Aberdeen to Inverness. Now owned by Pernod Ricard, Glentauchers has the same principal role it always had—supplying malt for blends.

◀ GLENTAUCHERS GORDON & MACPHAIL 1991

SINGLE MALT: SPEYSIDE
43% ABV

This 16-year-old Gordon & MacPhail bottling has a sweet, sherried character, with a subtle smoky flavor.

GLENTURRET

Scotland
Crieff, Perthshire
www.thefamousgrouse.com

This small Perthshire distillery, first licensed in 1775, claims to be the oldest working distillery in Scotland.

Today Glenturret is known as the spiritual home of The Famous Grouse *(see p119)*, an association showcased at its visitor center and its Famous Grouse Whisky School, which offers a one-day malt whisky course, including an in-depth distillery tour. Glenturret's other claim to fame is Towser, the cat, who won a place in *The Guinness Book of Records* for killing nearly 30,000 mice.

GLENTURRET 10-YEAR-OLD ►
SINGLE MALT: HIGHLANDS
40% ABV
Replacing the 12-year-old, this floral, vanilla-scented malt is now the main Glenturret expression.

GLENTURRET 14-YEAR-OLD
SINGLE MALT: HIGHLANDS
59.7% ABV
This limited-edition, cask-strength bottling has a molasseslike sweetness and notes of licorice.

GOLD COCK

Czech Republic
Jelinek Distillery,
Razov 472, 76312 Vizovice
www.rjelinek.cz

Jelinek Distillery was founded at the end of the 19th century, and acquired the Gold Cock brand from Tesetice, a Czech distillery that no longer exists. For its two expressions—Red Feathers and a 12-year-old—Jelinek uses Moravian barley and water is sourced from an underground well that is rich in minerals. The type of cask used is not specified.

◀ **GOLD COCK RED FEATHERS**
BLEND 40% ABV
Light and grainy, slightly metallic, and sweetish.

GOLDEN HORSE

Japan
Toa Shuzo, Chichibu
www.toashuzo.com

The Golden Horse brand is still owned by Toa Shuzo, the firm which used to own the Hanyu distillery *(see p175)*, and the whiskeys are drawn from its last remaining stocks. There are bottlings at 8, 10, and 12 years. They are rarely seen on the export markets and, at the time of writing, it is unclear what will happen to the Golden Horse brand once the Toa Shuzo stocks have disappeared.

GOLDEN HORSE 8-YEAR-OLD ▶
SINGLE MALT 40% ABV
A quite vibrant nose with light malt extract notes and some oak. There's a basic sweetness to this lightly perfumed malt, which has just a wisp of smoke on the finish, but a nagging acidic touch in some bottlings.

GOLDLYS

Belgium

Graanstokerij Filliers,
Leernsesteenweg 5, 9800 Deinze
www.filliers.be

The Flemish distiller Filliers has been making grain spirits since 1880. In 2008 it surprised the whiskey world by launching two whiskeys it had been maturing for years. Their name comes from the Lys River, which is nicknamed the "Golden River" because of the flax retted (soaked) in it. Goldlys uses malt, rye, and corn, and is distilled twice, first in a column still, then in a pot still—a process that is quite similar to that used to make bourbon. The spirit is then matured in former bourbon casks.

◀ GOLDLYS 10-YEAR-OLD
MIXED GRAIN WHISKEY
40% ABV
Spicy, sweet fruit, licorice, and a touch of wood. Some pepper in the short, dry finish.

GRAND MACNISH

Scotland
Owner: Macduff International

The long history of this brand dates back to Glasgow and 1863, when the original Robert McNish (an "a" crept into the brand name later), a grocer and general merchant, took up blending.

Grand Macnish Original still uses up to 40 whiskies in the blend, as was Robert McNish's practice. The distinctive bottle's label is graced by the McNish clan motto, *"Forti nihil difficile"* ("To the strong, nothing is difficult").

GRAND MACNISH ORIGINAL ▶
BLEND 40% ABV
Old leather and ripe fruits on the nose, giving way to a brandylike aroma. Noticeably sweet on the palate, with strong vanilla (wood) influences. A sustained and evolving finish, with some gentle smoke.

GRAND MACNISH 12-YEAR-OLD
BLEND 40% ABV
The extra age shows here in a fuller, rounder flavor with greater intensity and a more sustained finish.

GRANT'S

Scotland

Owner: William Grant & Sons

This staunchly independent company has prospered on Speyside since 1887, and remains in private hands. Today it is famous for Glenfiddich and its sister single malt, Balvenie, but it also produces a third malt, Kininvie, which is reserved for blending. In addition, it built a grain distillery at Girvan and a new single malt distillery, Ailsa Bay, also reserved for blending.

◄ GRANT'S FAMILY RESERVE

BLEND 40% ABV

An unmistakably Speyside nose, with fluting malty notes. A firm mouthfeel; banana-vanilla sweetness balances sharper malty notes. Clean, but very complex with a long, smooth finish.

GRANT'S 12-YEAR-OLD

BLEND 40% ABV

A blend of fine single malt and grain whiskies, matured in oak casks before being finished in ex-bourbon barrels. A warm and full-bodied Scotch of great richness is the result.

The company is determined to maintain close control over their supplies of whisky, and with good reason: Grant's Family Reserve blend broke through the 1 million case barrier as long ago as 1979. Grant's now sells around 4 million cases of whisky a year, and is one of the world's top five Scotch whisky brands, enjoyed in over 180 countries.

The blended range of whiskies continues to evolve, while still remaining true to the mark of quality associated with its distinctive triangular bottle.

GRANT'S ALE CASK RESERVE ▶

BLEND 40% ABV

Grant's has ventured into special wood finishes with great success. This is the only Scotch whisky to be finished in barrels that have previously held beer. Ale casks give the whisky a uniquely creamy, malty, and honeyed taste.

GRANT'S SHERRY CASK RESERVE

BLEND 40% ABV

Prepared in the same way as the ground-breaking ale cask version, but here the whisky is finished in Spanish Oloroso sherry casks, giving it a warm, rich, and fruity palate.

GREEN SPOT

Ireland

Midleton Distillery, Midleton, County Cork

In the days before distillers in Ireland spent millions on building brands, they simply used to make the stuff, leaving the filthy job of selling the whiskey to bonders like Mitchell's. This, of course, was a terrible business plan: it allowed the Scots to build global brands, while the Irish were obsessed with an ever-shrinking domestic market. By the time the Irish got back into the race in the 1960s, Irish whiskey had a miserable 1 percent of the global whiskey market. Green Spot is the last bonder's own label. Owned by Mitchell's of Dublin, it's a pure pot still whiskey, made in Midleton.

◀ **GREEN SPOT**

PURE POT STILL 40% ABV

Green Spot is matured for just six to eight years, but a glass of this is still bracing stuff, with a wonderful, lightly sherried finish. One of a kind.

GREENORE SINGLE GRAIN

Ireland

Cooley Distillery, Riverstown,
Cooley, County Louth
www.cooleywhiskey.com

Greenore is the only Irish single grain on sale. Produced in a continuous still instead of a pot still, grain whiskey is lighter in taste, but rougher on the back of the throat. For this reason, it is kept for blending. Greenore single grain whiskey is double-distilled, then matured in bourbon casks for at least eight years.

GREENORE SINGLE GRAIN 8-YEAR-OLD ▶

SINGLE GRAIN 40% ABV

This is a winner: a crackle of linseed on the nose and a peppery bite of firm cereal. No telltale "grain burn" at the end, but rather a sophisticated sprinkle of high-quality grated chocolate.

GREENORE SINGLE GRAIN 15-YEAR-OLD

SINGLE GRAIN 43% ABV

It's even more difficult to spot that this is a grain whiskey after 15 years in oak. With pronounced linseed notes and a minty coolness, there's an almost pot still quality to this classy whiskey.

GRÜNER HUND

Germany

Fleischmann, Bamberger Strasse 2,
91330 Eggolsheim-Neuses
www.fleischmann-whiskey.de

The Fleischmann brandy distillery was founded in 1980 on the premises of the original family company—a grocery and tobacco shop. In 1996, after nearly 14 years of experimentation with whiskey-distilling, the company launched their first whiskey expression. There are now seven single cask malt whiskeys available—Blaue Maus, Spinnaker, Krottentaler, Schwarzer Pirat, Grüner Hund, Austrasier, and Old Fahr—all bottled at 40% ABV.

◀ **GRÜNER HUND**
SINGLE MALT 51% ABV
Roasted almonds and cocoa on the nose. Dark chocolate, chiles, and gingerbread on the tongue, with a dry and medium-long finish.

GUILLON

France

Hameau de Vertuelle, 51150 Louvois, Champagne
www.whiskey-guillon.com

The Guillon Distillery is located in the Champagne region of France, and was purpose-built in 1997 to produce whiskey. It started distilling in 1999, distinguishing itself by the use of a variety of ex-wine casks for maturation. For the first maturation period, ex-Burgundy casks are used. After that, the whiskey is finished for six months in casks that used to contain sweet wines like Banyuls, Loupiac, and Sauternes. Guillon bottles a premium blend at 40% ABV. The various single malts are bottled at 42, 43, and 46% ABV.

GUILLON NO. 1 ▶
SINGLE MALT 46% ABV
Highly aromatic, fruity, and elegant, thanks to the unusual finish in sweet-wine casks.

HAIG

Scotland
Owner: Diageo

The distinguished name of Haig can trace its whisky-making pedigree back to the 17th century, when distilling began on the family farm. The company developed extensive interests in grain whisky distilling and was an early pioneer of blending. By 1919, however, it was absorbed into the DCL, where it continued to be a powerful force. The company's Dimple brand (known as Pinch in the US, *see p106*) was a highly successful deluxe expression, and Haig was once the bestselling whisky in the UK. But its glory days are far behind it: today, under the control of Diageo, it is found mainly in Greece and the Canary Islands.

◀ **HAIG**
BLEND 40% ABV
Some sweetness on the nose, with faint smoky notes. Light and delicate, with soft wood notes and some spice on the finish, where a hint of smoke returns.

HANCOCK'S RESERVE

USA

Buffalo Trace Distillery,
1001 Wilkinson Boulevard,
Frankfort, Kentucky
www.buffalotrace.com

This whiskey, which is usually created from barrels of spirit aged for around 10 years, takes its name from Hancock Taylor, great-uncle of US president Zachary Taylor, and an early surveyor of Kentucky. He was shot and killed by Native Americans in 1774, and it is said that his deathbed will was one of the first legal documents executed in the region.

HANCOCK'S RESERVE PRESIDENT'S SINGLE BARREL ▶

BOURBON 44.45% ABV

Oily on the nose, with licorice, caramel, and spicy rye. Sweet in the mouth, with malt, fudge, and vanilla notes. Drying in the finish, with oak notes, but the whiskey's residual sweetness remains to the end.

HANKEY BANNISTER

Scotland

Owner: Inver House Distillers

Founded by Messrs. Hankey and Bannister in 1757, the brand is now owned by Inver House Distillers, giving it access to a range of single malts from some of Scotland's most distinguished but lesser-known distilleries, such as Balblair, Balmenach, and Knockdhu. Key markets for Hankey Bannister include Latin America, Australia, and South America.

◀ HANKEY BANNISTER 21-YEAR-OLD

BLEND 43% ABV

A fresh and quite youthful nose. Soft and smooth, creamy toffee, with the vanilla house style coming through. Greater depth on the palate, with malty overtones and a warm finish.

HANKEY BANNISTER 40-YEAR-OLD

BLEND 43.3% ABV

Warm and fragrant aromas of raisin, chocolate, and citrus combine with spicy notes, leading to an exceptionally long-lasting, smooth, full-bodied finish.

HANYU

Japan

Distribution: Number One Drinks, Netherconesford, King Street, Norwich, UK
www.one-drinks.com

The Hanyu distillery was built by the Akuto family in the 1940s for producing *shochu*. Full production of whiskey began in 1980, and Hanyu enjoyed success until the financial crisis of 1996 triggered the end of the whiskey boom in Japan. The distillery had to close in 2000. When the firm was bought out in 2003, Ichiro Akuto was given a few months to buy back as much stock as he could before the distillery was demolished *(see Ichiro's Malt p187)*.

HANYU 1988 CASK 9501 ▶
SINGLE MALT 55.6% ABV
Vibrant and intense, with vanilla, some citrus, and a delicate cocoa-butter character. The Japanese oak adds a bittersweet edge. On the palate there's a rich depth. The finish shows smoke.

HAZELBURN

Scotland
Well Close, Campbeltown
www.springbankdistillers.com

Springbank Distillery is the great survivor of the Campbeltown whisky boom, which saw a staggering 34 distilleries in town in the 19th century. Today, Springbank is a mini-malt-whisky industry on its own, with three separate distillations under one roof: Springbank itself, the pungently smoky Longrow, and the light, gentle Hazelburn. As well as using no peat in its malt, Hazelburn—which was named after an old, abandoned distillery in Campbeltown—is triple-distilled. The first spirit was produced in 1997 and bottled as an 8-year-old in 2005. The 6,000 bottles released sold out within weeks.

◄ **HAZELBURN 8-YEAR-OLD**
SINGLE MALT: CAMPBELTOWN
46% ABV
Lowland in style, clean and refreshing, with a subtle, malty flavor.

HEAVEN HILL

USA

1701 West Breckinridge Street,
Louisville, Kentucky
www.heaven-hill.com

Heaven Hill is the USA's largest independent producer of distilled spirits to remain in family owner- ship. In 1996, the distillery and warehouses were almost completely destroyed by fire the company purchased Diageo's technologically advanced Bernheim Distillery in Louisville, and all production was moved to that site.

Heaven Hill's specialty is older, higher proof bourbons, traditional in character, full-bodied, and complex, such as Evan Williams *(see p115)* and Elijah Craig *(see p118)*, but its diverse portfolio also includes Bernheim Original *(see p48)*, Pikesville *(see p288)*, and Rittenhouse Rye *(see p300)*.

HEAVEN HILL ▶
BOURBON 40% ABV

An excellent and competitively priced "entry-level" bourbon, it has a nose of oranges and cornbread, a sweet, oily mouth-feel, and vanilla and corn featuring on the well-balanced palate.

HELLYERS ROAD

Australia
153 Old Surrey Road,
Burnie, Tasmania
www.hellyersroaddistillery.com.au

Hellyers Road opened in 1999 and is owned by the Betta Milk Cooperative. It now has about 3,000 ex-bourbon casks under maturation, and also produces a Tasmanian barley-based, pot-still vodka. The experience gained in running a milk processing plant has provided owner Laurie House with all the knowledge he needs to run this modern and highly automated plant.

The distillery is named after Henry Hellyer who, in the 1820s, built the first road into the interior of Tasmania, the same road that now leads to the distillery.

◄ HELLYERS ROAD ORIGINAL
SINGLE MALT 46.2% ABV
A light-bodied, pale-colored malt, un-tinted and non chill-filtered. The nose is fresh and citric, with vanilla notes.

HIGHLAND PARK

Scotland
Kirkwall, Orkney
www.highlandpark.co.uk

Nowadays, Highland Park's far-flung Orkney island location is a great asset for the marketing of its whiskies but, for much of its history, the distance from its core market—the big blenders on the mainland— represented a major challenge for the island distillery. It survived, and now produces a Highland malt that is highly regarded. ☛

HIGHLAND PARK 12-YEAR-OLD ▶
SINGLE MALT: ISLANDS
40% ABV
This whisky has all-around quality. There are soft heather-honey flavors, some richer spicy notes, and an enveloping wisp of peat smoke that leaves the finish quite dry.

HIGHLAND PARK 18-YEAR-OLD
SINGLE MALT: ISLANDS
43% ABV
This is a touch sweeter than the 12-year-old, with notes of heather, toffee, and polished leather. The flavor of peat smoke comes through stronger on the finish than on the palate.

HIGHLAND PARK

Having invested in the brand, its owners have ambitious plans to reach the top ten.

Highland Park was first licensed to David Robertson in 1798 but since 1937 it has been part of Highland Distilleries (now the Edrington Group). To this day, a proportion of the barley is malted using the distillery's original floor maltings. The malt is then dried in a kiln, using local peat, which has a slightly sweeter aroma than that from Islay.

◀ HIGHLAND PARK 30-YEAR-OLD

SINGLE MALT: ISLANDS
48.1% ABV

The flagship of the range. Caramel sweetness, aromatic spices, dark chocolate, and orange notes. A long, drying, smoky finish, tinged with salt.

HIGHLAND PARK 25-YEAR-OLD

SINGLE MALT: ISLANDS
48.1% ABV

The deep amber color reveals plenty of contact with European oak. In fact, half of it was matured in first-fill sherry butts. Despite its age, it has a rich, nutty flavor, with dried fruits and scented smoke.

HIGHWOOD

Canada
114 10th Avenue Southeast,
High River, Alberta
www.highwood-distillers.com

Unusually for Canada, Highwood, founded in 1974, is independently owned. It makes a range of spirits and is the only distillery in Canada using just wheat in its column stills as the base spirit for its blends. In 2005, it bought the Potter's and Cascadia distilleries. Potter's is a separate brand from Highwood. It is mixed with sherry, which adds another dimension to its flavor.

HIGHWOOD ▶
CANADIAN RYE 40% ABV
A blend of wheat and rye spirits. The oaky, vanilla-scented nose has traces of rye spice, orange blossom, and honey. The palate balances sweetness with oak tannins and nuts.

HIRSCH

Canada

Distribution: Preiss Imports Inc, San Diego, USA

This whiskey is no longer being made, but is still available via a US distributor. Although Canadian whiskey is often referred to as "rye," only a few brands contain more than 50 percent rye spirit, which is what makes it a true rye whiskey. Hirsch is one, and connoisseurs claim it rivals the best Kentucky ryes. The whiskeys are bottled in small batches, made in column stills, aged in ex-bourbon barrels, selected by Preiss Imports, and bottled by Glenora Distillers, Nova Scotia, which also produces a single malt called Glen Breton *(see p130)*.

◄ HIRSCH SELECTION 8-YEAR-OLD

CANADIAN RYE 43% ABV

Solvent and pine essence, then sweet maple sap on the nose. The taste is sweet, with caramel, dry coconut, and oak-wood; full-bodied. A bittersweet finish with a few earthy notes.

HIRSCH RESERVE

USA

Distribution: Preiss Imports
www.hirschbourbon.com

Hirsch Reserve is a drop of US whiskey history. The spirit itself was distilled in 1974 at Michter's Distillery, the last surviving one in Pennsylvania. Michter's closed in 1988, but one Adolf H. Hirsch had acquired a considerable stock of the spirit some years previously and, after it had been matured for 16 years, it was put into stainless steel tanks to prevent further aging. This whiskey is now available from Preiss Imports but, once gone, is gone forever.

HIRSCH RESERVE ▸
BOURBON 45.8% ABV
Caramel, honey, and rye dominate the complex nose, with a whiff of smoke also coming through. Oily corn, honey, and oak on the rich palate, with rye and more oak in the drying finish.

HOLLE

Switzerland
Hollen 52, 4426 Lauwil, Basel
www.single-malt.ch

Until July 1, 1999, it was strictly forbidden in Switzerland to distill spirit from grain, which was considered a food staple. After a change in the law, the Bader family, who had been making fruit spirits for a long time, started to distill from grains, and became the country's first whiskey producer.

◀ **HOLLE**
SINGLE MALT 42% ABV
Delicate aromas of malt, wood, and vanilla, with a flavor of wine. There are two varieties: one is matured in a white-wine cask, the other in a red-wine cask. A cask strength version is bottled at 51.1% ABV.

HUDSON

USA

Tuthilltown Distillery, 14 Gristmill Lane, Gardiner, New York
www.tuthilltown.com

In 1825, New York State had more than 1,000 working distilleries and produced a major share of the nation's whiskey. These days, Tuthilltown is New York's only remaining distillery. It was founded in 2001 by Brian Lee and Ralph Erenzo, and produces a quartet of "Hudson" bottlings, including a rich and full-flavored four-grain whiskey and a rich, caramel single malt, intended as an American "re-interpretation" of traditional Scottish whiskies.

HUDSON MANHATTAN RYE ▶
RYE WHISKEY 46% ABV
The first whiskey to be distilled in New York State for more than 80 years. Floral notes and a smooth finish on the palate, with a recognizable rye edge.

HUDSON BABY BOURBON
BOURBON 46% ABV
Made with 100 percent New York State corn, this is the first bourbon ever to be made in New York. It is a mildly sweet, smooth spirit with subtle hints of vanilla and caramel.

I.W. HARPER

USA

Four Roses Distillery,
1224 Bond Mills Road,
Lawrenceburg, Kentucky
www.fourroses.us

The historic and once bestselling I.W. Harper brand was established by Jewish businessman Isaac Wolfe Bernheim (1848–1945), a major figure in the bourbon business at the turn of the 20th century.

It was made at the Bernheim Distillery *(see p48)* in Louisville. It is now produced for current owners Diageo by Four Roses Distillery and is one of the leading bourbons in the Japanese market.

◀ **I.W. HARPER**

BOURBON 43% ABV

A big-bodied bourbon in which pepper combines with mint, oranges, caramel, and quite youthful charring on the nose, while caramel, apples, and oak feature on the elegant palate. The finish is dry and smoky.

ICHIRO'S MALT

Japan
Distribution: Number One Drinks, Netherconesford, King Street, Norwich, UK
www.one-drinks.com

Ichiro's Malt is a range of bottlings from Ichiro Akuto, who was the former president of Hanyu *(see p175)*, and the grandson of the founder, Isouji Akuto.

The whiskeys are drawn from the 400 casks of Hanyu single malt that Akuto managed to obtain after the Hanyu distillery was closed down. The bulk of Hanyu's remaining stock is being ☛

KING OF DIAMONDS, DISTILLED 1988, BOTTLED 2006 ▶

SINGLE MALT 56% ABV

Complex and nutty, with some dry burlap notes, sandalwood, citrus, pineapple, and pine. Spicy yet floral on the palate, with subtle smoke. One of the most highly complex in the series.

ACE OF DIAMONDS, DISTILLED 1986, BOTTLED 2008

SINGLE MALT 56.4% ABV

Mature nose, with Seville orange, furniture polish, rose, pipe tobacco, and when diluted, sloe and Moscatel. Spicy and chocolatey on the tongue.

ICHIRO'S MALT

☛ released by Akuto in a series of 53 whiskeys named after playing cards. This Card Series, as it is known, is memorable not only for its distinctive branding, but also for the high quality of many of its expressions.

The Card Series will be eked out until Akuto's new Chichibu single malt is fully established *(see p80)*. All of the bottlings are very limited, but some are available in export markets through distributors.

◀ FIVE OF SPADES, DISTILLED 2000, BOTTLED 2008

SINGLE MALT 60.5% ABV,

A sweet nose of sandalwood, light raisin, mint, dark chocolate, and some smoke. Water brings out baked muffins, an incenselike note, and white pepper.

ACE OF SPADES, DISTILLED 1985, BOTTLED 2006

SINGLE MALT 55% ABV

Sometimes called the Motorhead malt, after the band who sang *Ace of Spades*, this is one of the oldest in the Card Series. Bold, rich, and fat, with lots of raisin, some tarry notes, and molasses. The palate is chewy and toffeelike, with some prune and a savory finish.

IMPERIAL BLUE

India
Owner: Pernod Ricard
www.pernod-ricard.com

Imperial Blue is Pernod Ricard's second bestselling brand in India, at over 3.8 million cases a year. Previously a Seagram's brand (and still labeled as such), it benefited hugely from Pernod Ricard's acquisition of Seagram in 2001, jumping from producing under half a million cases to over a million by 2002. Imperial Blue hit the headlines in 2008 when some bottles in Andhra Pradesh were found to be understrength. It later transpired that they had been sabotaged by disgruntled workers.

IMPERIAL BLUE ▶
BLEND 42.8% ABV
In spite of the "grain" in its name, Imperial Blue is a blend of imported Scotch malt and locally made neutral spirit. It is light, sweet, and smooth.

INCHGOWER

Scotland
Buckie, Banffshire
www.malts.com

This is Speyside, but only just—the Inchgower Distillery sits near the mouth of the Spey and the fishing port of Buckie. It was established in 1871 by Alexander Wilson, using equipment from the disused Tochieneal Distillery, which had been founded in 1824 by his father, John Wilson, a short distance down the coast at Cullen. It remained a family business until 1930, when the stills went cold. Six years on, the local town council bought it for just £1,000, selling it on to Arthur Bell & Sons in 1938. Bell's blends swallow up most of the malt.

◀ INCHGOWER FLORA & FAUNA 14-YEAR-OLD
SINGLE MALT: SPEYSIDE
43% ABV
Brisk and fresh, with a floral nose, sweet-and-sour flavor, developing into a very short finish.

INISHOWEN

Ireland
Cooley Distillery, Riverstown,
Cooley, County Louth
www.cooleywhiskey.com

Inishowen is the kind of concept an accountant would come up with. It's brand economics by numbers. The Scotch industry is worth billions, with blended Scotch making up 90 percent of sales.

So if an Irish brand could create a similar product, it would have to be a sure-fire success—wouldn't it? There's nothing much wrong with Inishowen—it is well-made and nicely blended—it's just that it will never be... well, Scotch.

INISHOWEN ▶
BLEND 40% ABV
You won't find any other blended Irish whiskey that has a nose like this: it's both peaty and floral. However, it's the fine grain whiskey and not the malt that gives Inishowen some real charm.

INVER HOUSE GREEN PLAID

Scotland

Owner: Inver House Distillers

Controlled today by Thai Beverage, Inver House is one of the smaller but more dynamic Scotch whisky companies and, in 2008, was named International Distiller of the Year by *Whisky Magazine*. Its Green Plaid label was originally launched in 1956 in the US, where it remains among the top ten bestselling whiskies. More than 20 malts and grains are used to blend Green Plaid, which is available as a competitively priced non-aged version and as 12- and 21-year-olds. Inver House's Speyburn, anCnoc, Balblair, Old Pulteney, and Balmenach single malts undoubtedly feature strongly in the blend.

◄ **INVER HOUSE GREEN PLAID**

BLEND 40% ABV

A light, pleasant, undemanding dram, with notes of caramel and vanilla.

INVERGORDON

Scotland

Cottage Brae, Invergordon, Ross-shire
www.whyteandmackay.com

Located on the shores of the Moray Firth, the Invergordon grain distillery is owned by Whyte & Mackay. It was established in 1961 and expanded in 1963 and 1978. The distillery issued its pioneering official bottling of Invergordon Single Grain as a 10-year-old in 1991, but this was subsequently withdrawn. As a consequence, the only supplies now available are independent bottlings, many of which are very highly regarded by independent tasters.

INVERGORDON CLAN DENNY 1966 ▶
SINGLE GRAIN 49.8% ABV
The independent bottlings of Invergordon are uniformly old (typically 38–42 years), and are characterized by a sweet nose and creamy texture. Expect notes of vanilla and wood, and spices such as cinnamon and nutmeg.

THE IRISHMAN

Ireland

www.hotirishman.com

Bernard Walsh's The Irishman range includes two core offerings and a special release. The single malt uses whiskey from Bushmills, and is a vatting of whiskey matured in bourbon and sherry casks. The second core release is the Irishman 70, which is a more innovative concoction. The 70 in the title refers to the percentage of Bushmills malt in the bottle. The remaining 30 percent is pure pot still from Midleton. There is no grain whiskey used in this range.

◀ THE IRISHMAN SINGLE MALT

SINGLE MALT 40% ABV

Bushmills tends to keep all the best whiskey for itself, which means this malt has great cereal character but will never be outstanding. There is a hint of sherry on the palate, but this could have done with a bit longer in the cask.

THE IRISHMAN 70

PURE POT STILL / MALT BLEND 40% ABV

The combination of malt and pot still is intriguing, offering a direct hit of dried fruit and rich, almost burned sugar.

ISLAY MIST

Ireland
Owner: MacDuff International

Created in 1922 for the 21st birthday of the son of the Laird of Islay House, Islay Mist is a highly awarded blend of single malts from the Hebridean island. The strongly flavored Laphroaig is predominant, but is tempered with Speyside and Highland malts. Naturally, Islay Mist is favored by lovers of peat-flavored whiskies, but it also offers an excellent alternative to less characterful blends. It is produced by MacDuff International, and is available in standard, deluxe, 8-year-old, and 17-year-old versions. The latter two use identical blend recipes; the difference is the age.

ISLAY MIST DELUXE ▶
BLEND 40% ABV
A great smoky session whisky that some will find easier to drink than full-on Islay malt. Sweet and complex under all the peat.

J&B

Scotland
Owner: Diageo

A Diageo brand widely sold in Spain, France, Portugal, Turkey, South Africa, and the US, J&B is one of the world's top-selling blended whiskies.

The founding firm dates from 1749. In 1831 it was bought by the entrepreneurial Alfred Brooks, who renamed it Justerini and Brooks. The company began blending in the 1880s, and developed J&B Rare in the 1930s, when the end of Prohibition in the US created a demand for lighter-colored whisky with a more delicate flavor.

◄ J&B RARE
BLEND 40% ABV
Top-class single malts such as Knockando, Auchroisk, and Glen Spey are at its heart; delicate smokiness suggests an Islay influence. Apple and pear sweetness, vanilla, and honey against a background of restrained peat.

J&B JET
BLEND 40% ABV
A very mellow, smooth whisky, with Speyside malt at its core.

JACK DANIEL'S

USA

280 Lynchburg Road,
Lynchburg, Tennessee
www.jackdaniels.com

Jack Daniel's has become an iconic brand worldwide. Its founder, Jasper Newton "Jack" Daniel reputedly started to make whiskey as a child, and by 1860 was running his own distilling business at the tender age of 14.

Today, Jack Daniel's is owned by the Kentucky-based Brown-Forman Corporation.

JACK DANIEL'S OLD NO. 7 ▶
TENNESSEE WHISKEY 40% ABV
Powerful nose of vanilla, smoke, and licorice. On the palate, oily cough-mixture and molasses, with a final kick of maple syrup and burnt wood lingering in the finish. Not particularly complex, but muscular and distinctive.

JACK DANIEL'S SINGLE BARREL
TENNESSEE WHISKEY 47% ABV
Charming and smooth on the nose, with notes of peach, vanilla, nuts, and oak. The comparatively dry palate offers depth, richness, and elegance, with oily corn, licorice, malt, and oak. Malt and oak linger in the lengthy finish, along with a touch of rye spice.

JAMES MARTIN'S

Scotland
Owner: Glenmorangie

The James Martin name relates to the Leith blenders MacDonald Martin Distillers (now Glenmorangie,) and dates back to 1878, when the original James Martin set up in business. Presented in stylish Art Deco bottles, the blend was always highly regarded, as it contained a healthy share of Glenmorangie single malt with some richer components.

Currently there are 12- and 20-year-old versions of James Martin's, while bottles of the 30-year-old can still be bought from specialist retailers.

◄ JAMES MARTIN'S 20-YEAR-OLD
BLEND 40% ABV
Citrus on the nose initially, then honey, vanilla, and a rich mead liqueur. With water, hints of coconut and vanilla appear. Very soft on the palate at the start, with cereal (grain) notes to the fore. Complex, lively spice and soft, sweet grain notes. Well-balanced with a soft finish.

JAMESON

Ireland
Midleton Distillery,
Midleton, County Cork
www.jamesonwhiskey.com

This is the biggest-selling Irish whiskey. The standard blend is a 50:50 blend of medium-bodied pot still and grain whiskey. It's a light spirit that lacks character. Beyond the standard bottling, though, are some cracking whiskeys. Gold Reserve was originally launched as a premium, duty-free blend, but it is now widely available. Some of the whiskeys used in it are more than 20 years old, but they ☛

JAMESON ▶
BLEND 40% ABV
The malty smell is promising, but the drink itself is a let-down. The grain is unruly and overwhelms the pot-still, leaving some citrus notes. There is a gentle buzz of sherry—nothing more.

JAMESON GOLD RESERVE
BLEND 43% ABV
This is a viscous, oily, syrupy mouth-coater of a whiskey. Finer, lighter flavors find it hard to fight their way through the fug of sugars. The finish is buzzy and long, in rather the same way as a cough medicine.

JAMESON

are cut with younger pot still whiskey, matured in first-fill oak casks. This is the only Irish whiskey to feature virgin wood, giving the blend a sweet, vanillalike flavor.

Jameson's Special Reserve 12-year-old stays in Oloroso sherry butts for 12 years and has won several awards. Six extra years in the cask doesn't change the flavor profile of the 18-year-old premium offering much, but it does double the price.

◀ JAMESON SPECIAL RESERVE 12-YEAR-OLD

BLEND 40% ABV

A world-beating whiskey. Hints of leather and spice on the nose and an incredibly silky quality in the mouth. Dried fruits wrapped in milk chocolate round off a master-class in how to make a great whiskey.

JAMESON LIMITED RESERVE 18-YEAR-OLD

BLEND 40% ABV

The pot still here has taken old age well. The body is firm and yielding and the Oloroso wood has to be very fine not to dominate a blend this old. Sweet almond and spiced fudge notes complement the oiliness of the pot still.

JEFFERSON'S

USA

McLain & Kyne Ltd. (Castle Brands), Louisville, Kentucky
www.mclainandkyne.com

The Louisville company of McLain & Kyne, Ltd. was formed by Trey Zoeller to carry on the distilling traditions of his ancestors. McLain & Kyne specializes in premium, very small-batch bourbons, most notably Jefferson's and Sam Houston *(see p309)*.

JEFFERSON'S SMALL BATCH 8-YEAR-OLD ▶

BOURBON (VARIABLE ABV)

This bourbon has been aged in the heart of metal-clad warehouses to accentuate the extreme temperatures of Kentucky, forcing the bourbon to expand deep into the barrel and extract desirable flavors from the wood. The nose is fresh, with vanilla and ripe peach notes, while the smooth, sweet palate boasts more vanilla, caramel, and berries. The finish is very delicate, with toasted vanilla and cream.

Whiskey Tour: Ireland

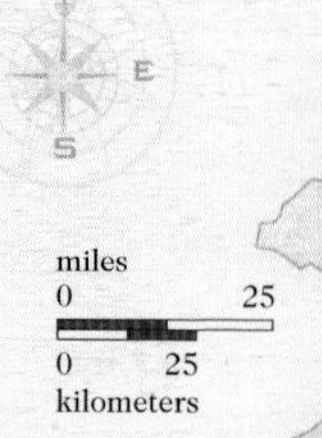

In 1887, when the Victorian travel and drinks writer Alfred Barnard visited Ireland, he had 28 different distilleries to visit. Nowadays, the range is more limited, but every bit as enjoyable. Several historic whiskey distilleries have facilities for tourists, and there are other attractions and the beautiful Irish landscape to explore.

DAY 1: GIANTS CAUSEWAY, BUSHMILLS

❶ Start your trip at the magnificent **Giants Causeway**, a World Heritage Site near the town of Bushmills, where extraordinary hexagonal basalt columns stretch out along the rugged coast.

❷ Of all the Irish distilleries that are open to the public, **Bushmills** is the only one that is still in production. Enjoy the tour, sample some fine whiskeys, then stay at the nearby Bushmills Inn for some great food and a good night's sleep.

GIANTS CAUSEWAY

DAY 2: COOLEY, OLD JAMESON DISTILLERY

COOLEY DISTILLERY

❸ Although **Cooley** Distillery is not open to the public, the nearby hills and the seaside town of Greenore are worth seeing on the way to Dublin.

❹ Avoid the Dublin traffic by taking the LUAS tram from Junction 9 of the M50 to Smithfield in the city center. This is near the **Old Jameson Distillery**, which offers guided tours and the chance to sample Jameson whiskey.

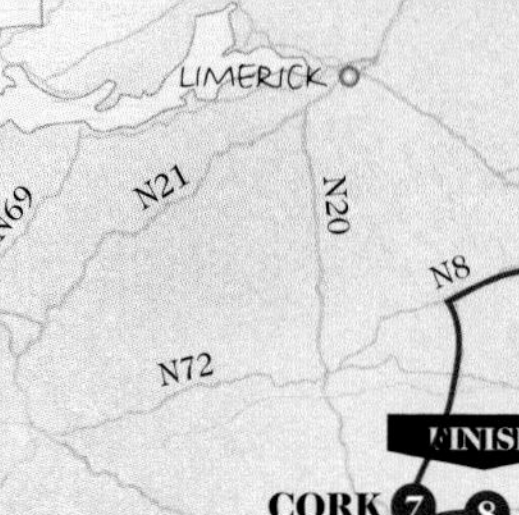

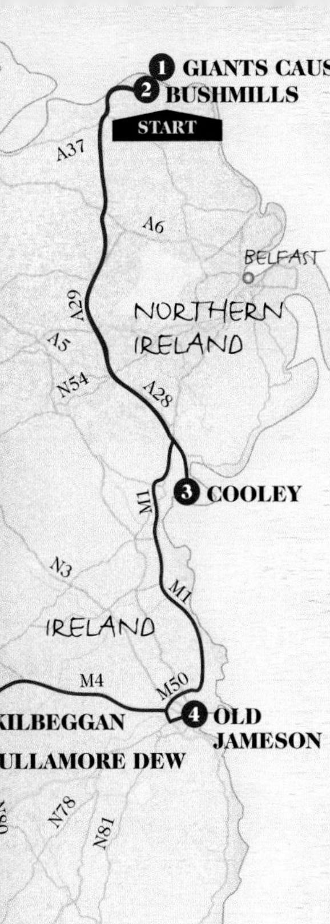

DAY 3: KILBEGGAN, TULLAMORE DEW

5 Take Junction 7 of the M50 and head west out of Dublin to the old Locke's building at **Kilbeggan**. The original distillery fell silent in 1957, but the site has been revived by locals and now houses the Kilbeggan micro-distillery and a whiskey museum with working waterwheel, restaurant, shop, and whiskey bar. Cooley leases warehouses at this site and matures some whiskeys here.

KILBEGGAN

The vibrant town of Tullamore is home to the **Tullamore Dew Heritage Centre**. This building used to be a bonded warehouse for storing whiskey casks before they were shipped downstream to Dublin, and is now the setting for an exhibition about traditional whiskey-making. Tullamore Dew whiskey is distilled at Midleton these days, but is, of course, available for tasting at the heritage center.

DAY 4: CORK, THE JAMESON EXPERIENCE AT MIDLETON

7 The cross-country trip from Tullamore to Cork traverses the boggy heart of Ireland—a bleak landscape that is strangely beautiful at any time of the year. **Cork** city is a food haven, where you can visit the historic English Market to buy a picnic lunch, or perhaps try the Market Café for local specialties. For a drink, stop at the South County Bar & Café, in Douglas Village, a suburb of Cork. It's a traditional pub with its own "whiskey corner" to celebrate Irish whiskey.

POT STILL AT MIDLETON

8 **The Jameson Experience** is set in the beautifully restored 18th-century distillery at Midleton, and boasts the world's largest pot still, which now stands outside the buildings. For refreshment, try the restaurant at nearby Ballymaloe House, which is overseen by Darina Allen, the doyen of Irish foodies.

TOUR STATISTICS

DAYS: 4
LENGTH: 375 miles (600km)
TRAVEL: Car, tram, walking
DISTILLERIES: 1 working, 3 converted

JIM BEAM

USA

149 Happy Hollow Road,
Clermont, Kentucky
www.jimbeam.com

Jim Beam is the bestselling bourbon brand in the world. Its origins date back to the 18th century, when German-born farmer and miller Jacob Boehm traveled west into Bourbon County, Kentucky, from Virginia, carrying with him his copper pot still. He is reputed to have sold his first barrel of whiskey for cash in 1795, and subsequently moved

◀ JIM BEAM WHITE LABEL 4-YEAR-OLD

BOURBON 40% ABV

Vanilla and delicate floral notes on the nose. Initially sweet, with restrained vanilla, then drier, oaky notes develop, fading into furniture polish and soft malt in the finish.

JIM BEAM CHOICE 5-YEAR-OLD

BOURBON 40% ABV

Charcoal-filtered in the style of Tennessee whiskeys after maturation. Soft and silky in character, with more caramel notes than other expressions.

his distilling operation into Washington County when he inherited land there.

Jim (James Beauregard) Beam himself was Jacob Boehm's great-grandson. He joined the family business at the age of 16, in 1880, and trade prospered in the years before Prohibition forced the closure of the distillery.

Jim Beam founded the present Clermont Distillery soon after the repeal of Prohibition in 1933, despite being 70 years old at the time. He died in 1947, five years after "Jim Beam" first appeared on the bottle label, and two years after the firm had been sold to Harry Blum of Chicago, previously a partner in the company.

JIM BEAM BLACK LABEL 8-YEAR-OLD ▶

BOURBON 43% ABV

Greater depth than White Label, with more complex fruit and vanilla notes, plus licorice and sweet rye.

JIM BEAM RYE

RYE WHISKEY 40% ABV

Light, perfumed, and aromatic on the nose, with lemon and mint. Oily in the mouth, with soft fruits, honey, and rye. Drying and spicy in the finish.

JOHNNIE WALKER

Scotland

Owner: Diageo

While the original firm can be traced back to the purchase of a Kilmarnock grocery store in 1820, Walker's did not enter the whisky business in a serious way until the 1860s. Then, John Walker's son and grandson progressively launched and developed their range of whiskies. These were based around the original Walker's Old Highland blend, which was launched in 1865 and is the

◄ JOHNNIE WALKER BLACK LABEL

BLEND 40% ABV

The flagship, classic blend, recognizable by the smoky kick contributed by Talisker, Caol Ila, and Lagavulin. Glendullan and Mortlach add some Speyside malt.

JOHNNIE WALKER GREEN LABEL

BLENDED MALT 43% ABV

Complex, rich, and powerful. Pepper and oak, fruit aromas, a malty sweetness, and some smoke.

ancestor of today's Black Label. In 1925 the firm joined DCL and, by 1945, Johnnie Walker was the world's bestselling brand of Scotch.

The range comprises Johnnie Walker Red, Black, Gold, Blue, Blue Label King George V, and Green Label. From time to time the firm also releases one-off, limited, or regional expressions. In recent years there has been a trend to move the brand upmarket. When Blue Label was launched in 1992, it set new price records for blended whisky. This was followed by the King George V Edition, which cost three times as much as the Blue, and the ultra-exclusive 1805, sold at £1,000 a single glass.

JOHNNIE WALKER GOLD LABEL ▶

BLEND 40% ABV

Honey, fresh fruit, and toffee notes, with smoke in the background. Diageo recommends chilling this in the freezer before serving.

JOHNNIE WALKER BLUE LABEL

BLEND 40% ABV

Smooth and mellow, with traces of spice, honey, and the signature hint of smoke.

JOHNNY DRUM

USA

Kentucky Bourbon Distillers,
1869 Loretto Road,
Bardstown, Kentucky
www.kentuckybourbonwhiskey.com

Johnny Drum is said to have been a Confederate drummer boy during the Civil War, and later a pioneer farmer and distiller in Kentucky. Johnny Drum bourbon was formerly produced in the Willet Distillery near Bardstown, but this closed in the early 1980s when the last of the Willet family members retired. The plant was acquired by Kentucky Bourbon Distillers, Ltd., for whom a range of whiskeys is distilled under contract.

◄ **JOHNNY DRUM**

BOURBON (VARIABLE ABV)

Smooth and elegant on the nose, with vanilla, gentle spices, and smoke. This is a full-bodied bourbon, well-balanced and smooth in the mouth, with vanilla and a hint of smoke. The finish is lingering and sophisticated.

JURA

Scotland
Isle of Jura, Argyllshire
www.isleofjura.com

When two estate owners on Jura resurrected the Jura distillery in the late 1950s, half a century after it had fallen into disuse, the profile of the whisky changed. Gone was the strong, phenolic malt of the past, and in came something more Highland in style, with less peat and a more subtle touch.

In recent years Jura has also produced an array of limited-edition bottlings, some of which have been quite heavily peated.

JURA 10-YEAR-OLD ▶
SINGLE MALT: ISLANDS
40% ABV
A lightly peated island malt that seems to have improved in recent years.

JURA SUPERSTITION
SINGLE MALT: ISLANDS
43% ABV
A mix of heavily peated, young Jura with older whisky, to produce an intensely smoky, smooth-textured malt.

KAVALAN

Taiwan

King Car Kavalan Distillery,
Yuanshan, Yi-lan County
www.kavalanwhisky.com

Situated on Yi-lan Plain, in the northeast of Taiwan, Kavalan is proudly named by the founder, Mr. T.T. Lee, after the indigenous people of the plain.

The distillery was built in 2006 and has the capacity to produce 858,000 gallons (3.9 million liters) per annum. The intense heat and humidity of the site greatly speeds up maturation and increases evaporation. Under such circumstances, the whiskey is fully mature after two to three years.

Kavalan was first bottled in 2008. There are now four expressions available, and they are all excellent.

◀ **KAVALAN CLASSIC**
SINGLE MALT 40% ABV
Light and fruity on the nose, led by tropical fruits (mango, papaya) and ripe peaches. Light bodied, the taste is sweet, with fresh acidity, drying in the medium-length finish. With water a trace of fennel appears, and peach-cream and chocolate in the aftertaste.

KENTUCKY GENTLEMAN

USA

Tom Moore Distillery, 1 Barton Road, Bardstown, Kentucky

Kentucky Gentleman is offered both as a blended whiskey and as a straight bourbon. According to its producers, the blended version is created from a blend of Kentucky straight bourbon whiskey and spirits from the finest grains.

The popular straight expression enjoys a notably loyal following in the southern states, particularly Florida, Alabama, and Virginia. It is produced at the Tom Moore Distillery, Bardstown, which was controlled by Barton Brands until 2009, when it was sold to the New Orleans-based Sazerac Company.

KENTUCKY GENTLEMAN ▶
BOURBON 40% ABV

Made with a higher percentage of rye than most whiskeys made at Tom Moore, this offers caramel and sweet oak aromas, and is oily, full-bodied, spicy, and fruity in the mouth. Rye, fruits, vanilla, and cocoa figure in the lingering, flavorful, and comparatively assertive finish.

KESSLER

USA

Jim Beam Distillery,
149 Happy Hollow Road,
Clermont, Kentucky
www.jimbeam.com

One of the best-known and most highly regarded blended American whiskeys, Kessler traces its origins back to 1888, when it was first blended by one Julius Kessler, who traveled from saloon to saloon across the West, selling his whiskey as he went.

◄ **KESSLER**

BLEND 40% ABV

Kessler has carried the slogan "Smooth as Silk" for more than half a century, and it certainly lives up to its name. The nose is light and fruity, and the palate sweet, with just enough complexity of licorice and leather to highlight the fact that the bourbon in this blend was aged for a minimum of four years.

KILBEGGAN

Ireland
The Old Kilbeggan Distillery, Main Street, Kilbeggan, County Westmeath
www.kilbegganwhiskey.com

In the mid-1950s, the most famous of the distilleries, John Locke & Sons, fell silent. Although the two remaining Locke family members —sisters Flo and Sweet—had warehouses full of raw ingredients, they had no interest in whiskey-making. With post-war whiskey prices on the rise, they decided to sell the distillery.

Nowadays, Kilbeggan whiskeys are Cooley blends, distilled in County Louth, but the spirits are still matured and bottled on site.

KILBEGGAN ▶
BLEND 40% ABV
A grainy blend, with strong notes of honey and oatmeal. The end note is a pleasing combination of coffee and dark chocolate.

KILBEGGAN 15-YEAR-OLD
BLEND 40% ABV
Age can thin and fracture a whiskey, or it can be its making. The Kilbeggan 15-year-old blend is spectacular. Expect the usual Cooley honey and cookie notes, distilled to perfection.

KILCHOMAN

Scotland
Rockside Farm, Bruichladdich, Islay
www.kilchomandistillery.com

Whisky-making began here in 2005, and this is as quintessential a farm distillery as you'll find. The barley is grown on Rockside Farm, and malting, fermenting, distilling, and maturing all take place on-site; a dam on the farm creates a supply of fresh water. At the time of writing, Kilchoman was yet to bottle its first whisky, but they do sell New Spirit. Matured in bourbon casks for about five months, this isn't technically new make, but then neither is it whisky yet either. It does, though, offer a signpost to the kind of whisky that will one day issue forth from the Kilchoman warehouse.

◀ **KILCHOMAN NEW SPIRIT**
NEW MAKE SPIRIT 63.5% ABV
A light wave of peat on the nose, but essentially fruity and fresh. There's a butterscotch sweetness too.

KIRIN GOTEMBA

Japan
Shibanta 970, Gotembashi, Shizuoka
www.kirin.co.jp

Kirin's Gotemba distillery was built in 1973 as part of a joint venture with the former Canadian giant Seagram *(see p313)*. Its output is much in line with the light flavors preferred by the Japanese consumer in the 1970s. That said, the distillery had to supply all the needs of Kirin's blends, so it made three grain whiskeys and three styles of malt.

GOTEMBA FUJISANROKU 18-YEAR-OLD ▶
SINGLE MALT 40% ABV
More floral and restrained than the "old" Fuji Gotemba 18-year-old, with less of the oakiness. Some peach, lily, and a zesty grapefruit note. The honey found in the grain reappears here.

FUJI GOTEMBA 15-YEAR-OLD
SINGLE GRAIN 40% ABV
A very sweet and concentrated nose, almost liqueurlike in its syrupy, honeyed unctuousness. There are touches of sesame, coconut, and orange zest. The palate is soft and gentle with a melting butter quality. The finish balances oak and sweetness.

KIRIN KARUIZAWA

Japan
Maseguchi 1795–2, Oaza, Miyotamachi, Kitasakugun, Nagano
www.kirin.co.jp

This former winery was converted to whiskey-making in the 1950s. To get its big-hitting and smoky style, it retains techniques that are rare now even in Scotland: the heaviness of the Golden Promise strain of barley used is accentuated by the small stills, while maturation in ex-sherry casks adds a dried-fruit character.

◀ KARUIZAWA 1995: NOH SERIES, BOTTLED 2008

SINGLE MALT 63% ABV

Hugely resinous nose that mixes tiger balm, geranium, boot polish, prune, and oiled woods. Lightly astringent palate that needs water to release the tannic grip. An exotic, floral whiskey.

KARUIZAWA 1986: CASK NO. 7387, BOTTLED 2008

SINGLE MALT 60.7% ABV

Incense on the nose along with wax, crystallized fruits, dried fig, porcini, cassia, tamarind paste, smoke, and spice. The palate needs water to bring forth dried fruits, rosewood, and coffee.

KNAPPOGUE CASTLE

Ireland
Bushmills Distillery, 2 Distillery Road, County Antrim

After World War II, the owner of Knappogue Castle took to buying casks of whiskey, which he would store in a cellar. These whiskeys would then be bottled and given away to family and friends over time. The last of these original casks, filled with Tullamore whiskey, was bottled in 1987.

In the 1990s the son of the castle's owner, Mark Andrews, decided to follow suit and bottle single vintages of his own, also labeled Knappogue Castle.

The first of these were created from whiskey produced at Cooley Distillery, but the more recent vintages come from Bushmills.

KNAPPOGUE CASTLE 1995 ▶
SINGLE MALT 40% ABV
Clearly originates from a Bushmills malt, and a classy one to boot. There are notes of toasted nuts, while a juicy, honey sweetness lingers on the palate. It is still too young, though, to display the full potential of its characteristics.

KNOB CREEK

USA

Jim Beam Distillery,
149 Happy Hollow Road,
Clermont, Kentucky
www.jimbeam.com

Knob Creek is the Kentucky town where Abraham Lincoln's father, Thomas, owned a farm and worked at the local distillery. This bourbon is one of three introduced in 1992, when Jim Beam launched its Small Batch Bourbon Collection. It is made to the same high-rye formula as the Jim Beam-distilled Basil Hayden's *(see p39)* and Old Grand-Dad *(see p276)* brands.

◄ KNOB CREEK 9-YEAR-OLD
BOURBON 50% ABV
Knob Creek has a nutty nose of sweet, tangy fruit and rye, with malt, spice, and nuts on the fruity palate, drying in the finish with notes of vanilla.

KNOCKANDO

Scotland
Knockando, Morayshire
www.malts.com

Knockando was launched as a single malt in the late 1970s. Most of the distillery's production has tended to go into J&B.

Established in 1898, the distillery was only run on a seasonal basis and soon fell victim to the speculative crash that hit the industry at the beginning of the 20th century. Knockando was snapped up by the London gin distillers Gilbey's, who, via a series of acquisitions, became part of what is now Diageo. In 1968, the floor maltings were stopped and the old malt barns converted to host meetings for J&B salesmen.

KNOCKANDO 12-YEAR-OLD ▶
SINGLE MALT: SPEYSIDE
43% ABV
This gentle, grassy malt has a cereal character and a light, creamy texture.

KNOCKANDO 18-YEAR-OLD
SINGLE MALT: SPEYSIDE
43% ABV
A slightly more fulsome expression, with a smooth, mellow texture.

KNOCKEEN HILLS

Ireland

www.irish-poteen.com

Poteen (or poitín) is a clear spirit that was traditionally distilled in homemade pot stills throughout Ireland. It was first made with malted barley or any available grain, or sometimes potatoes.

One of the few to survive is Knockeen Hills. Its spirit is bottled at three strengths: triple-distilled at 60% and 70% ABV, and quadruple-distilled at 90% ABV. It should not be drunk neat.

◄ KNOCKEEN HILLS 60

POTEEN 60% ABV

Clean, fresh, and fruity on the nose. Creamy textured, with tantalizing sweet and juicy fruit notes on the palate. Crisp, mouth-cleansing finish.

KNOCKEEN HILLS 70

POTEEN 70% ABV

Stronger on the nose than the 60. With a large measure of water (almost 50:50), it becomes fruity, with tangerine-skin aromas and a sweet perfumed note. Warming in the mouth, sweet and sour on the palate, witha dry, fruit-tinged finish.

LADYBURN

Scotland

Owner: William Grant & Sons

Now long-since closed, Ladyburn was a malt distillery within a huge grain distillery in Girvan on the Ayrshire coast. Its owners, William Grant & Sons, moved into grain whisky in 1964, when DCL threatened to stop supplying them with grain spirit for its blends. Two years later, in 1966, it created Ladyburn on the site. It only ran for nine years before being converted into a vodka distillery in 1975, so single malt bottlings are very rare. Despite this, official bottlings, as well as independents, continue to be eked out of the remaining stocks, and there are rumors that the owners kept back 30 casks to release as and when they choose.

LADYBURN 1973 ▸

SINGLE MALT: LOWLANDS
50.4% ABV

A limited-release bottling, with a mellow, oaky character and delicious vanilla sweetness.

LAGAVULIN

Scotland
Port Ellen, Isle of Islay
www.malts.com

Lagavulin is said to have evolved into a distillery from various illicit smuggling botheys in 1817. In 1836 its lease was taken over by Alexander Graham, who sold the island's whiskies through his shop in Glasgow. Peter Mackie, the nephew of Graham's partner, worked for the business and went on to create the famous White Horse blend based on Islay malt. When Laphroaig refused to supply him, he built Malt Mill Distillery in the grounds of Lagavulin—inherited after his uncle's death.

◄ LAGAVULIN 16-YEAR-OLD
SINGLE MALT: ISLAY 43% ABV
Intensely smoky nose with the scent of seaweed and iodine and a sweetness in the mouth that dries to a peaty finish.

LAGAVULIN 12-YEAR-OLD
SINGLE MALT: ISLAY 56.4% ABV
An initial sweetness gives way to scented smoke and a malty, fruity flavor ahead of the dry, peaty finish.

Malt Mill was demolished in the 1960s, but Lagavulin rode on the back of the White Horse until its iconic 16-year-old became a founding member of the "Classic Malts" in 1988.

During the slump in demand for Scotch in the 1980s, Lagavulin was working a two- to three-day week. Sixteen years down the line, the managers were having to juggle the short supply with booming demand. To try and meet demand, production at Lagavulin was cranked up to a seven-day week, and less and less was made available for blends. It is said that over 85 percent of Lagavulin is now bottled as a single malt.

LAGAVULIN DISTILLERS EDITION ▶

SINGLE MALT: ISLAY 43% ABV

A richer, fuller-flavored take on the 16-year-old, still with plenty of dense smoke and seaweed.

LAGAVULIN 21-YEAR-OLD

SINGLE MALT: ISLAY 56.5% ABV

Pungent and smoky on one hand, a sherried, syrupy warmth on the other. The two sides live in harmony.

LAMMERLAW

New Zealand
Bottled by Cadenhead
www.wmcadenhead.com

In 1974, the Wilson Brewery and Malt Extract Company produced New Zealand's first legal whiskey for 100 years. Unfortunately, its pot stills were made from stainless steel, and the spirit was horrible. In 1981, the distillery was acquired by Seagram, who vastly improved quality and produced a 10-year-old single malt—Lammerlaw—named after the nearby mountain range. The distillery was dismantled in 2002, and the casks passed to Milford's owners (*see p256*). Cadenhead has bottled Lammerlaw in its World Whiskies series.

◀ **CADENHEAD'S LAMMERLAW 10-YEAR-OLD**
SINGLE MALT 47.3% ABV
Light-bodied and somewhat "green" and cereal-like, but pleasant to taste.

LANGS

Scotland
Owner: Ian MacLeod
www.ianmacleod.com

At the heart of this blend is Glengoyne single malt, from the distillery outside Glasgow. This was bought in 1876 by two local merchants, Alexander and Gavin Lang. Brand and distillery were later sold to Robertson & Baxter.

The subsequent sale to Ian MacLeod marked an important transition for that business, from blender and bottler to distiller. Today, the principal Langs products are Langs Select 12-year-old and Langs Supreme.

LANGS SUPREME ▶
BLEND 40% ABV
A rich malt aroma on the nose, well-matured, with just a hint of sherry. A full-flavored, medium-sweet blend, with the Glengoyne heart evident.

LANGS SELECT 12-YEAR-OLD
BLEND 40% ABV
Rhubarb, cooking apples, and plenty of vanilla on the nose. Richer on the palate, with lots of fruity notes and a lemon-tart sweetness that build toward a spicy finish with hints of peat smoke.

LAPHROAIG

Scotland
Port Ellen, Isle of Islay
www.laphroaig.com

Laphroaig has always reveled in its pungent smokiness—a mix of hemp, carbolic soap, and bonfire that is about as a far from the creamy, cocktail end of whisky as it is possible to get. Its intense medicinal character is said to be one reason it was among the few Scotch whiskies allowed into the US during Prohibition—it was accepted as a "medicinal spirit,"

◀ LAPHROAIG 10-YEAR-OLD CASK STRENGTH
SINGLE MALT: ISLAY
57.3% ABV
Tar, seaweed, and salt, and some sweet wood too. Iodine and hot peat rumble through a long, dramatic finish.

LAPHROAIG10-YEAR-OLD
SINGLE MALT: ISLAY
40% ABV
The 10-year-old is also very popular. Beneath the dense peat smoke and salty sea spray is a refreshing, youthful malt with a sweet core.

and could be obtained with a prescription from a doctor.

Laphroaig was founded in 1810 by Alexander and Donald Johnston, although official production did not begin for five years. Living beside the equally famous Lagavulin has not always been easy, and there were the usual fights over water access, but today the feeling is more one of mutual respect.

Laphroaig is one of the very few distilleries to have retained its floor maltings, which supply about a fifth of its needs.

LAPHROAIG QUARTER CASK ▶
SINGLE MALT: ISLAY
48% ABV
The Quarter Cask is at the heart of Laphroaig's core range. Small casks speed up the maturation process and lead to a sweet, woody taste that succumbs to a triumphal burst of peat smoke.

LAPHROAIG 25-YEAR-OLD
SINGLE MALT: ISLAY
50.9% ABV
A spicy, floral character, with smoke and sea spray taking over only in the finish. Also available in cask strength.

LARK

Australia
14 Davey Street, Hobart, Tasmania
www.larkdistillery.com.au

The modern revival of whiskey-making in Australia began in Tasmania, with the opening of this small distillery in Hobart in 1992. It was the brainchild of Bill Lark, who realized that the island has all the right ingredients: plenty of rich barley fields, abundant pure, soft water, peat bogs, and a perfect climate for maturation.

Lark is now assisted by his wife Lyn and daughter Kristy. They use locally grown Franklin barley, 50 percent of it re-dried over peat. The malt is bottled from single casks at three to five years.

◀ LARK'S SINGLE MALT
SINGLE MALT 58% ABV
Malty and lightly peated, with peppery notes. A smooth mouthfeel, with rich malt, apples, and oak-wood, and some spice in the finish.

LARK'S PM
BLENDED MALT 45% ABV
Sweet and smoky on the nose and palate; clean and lightly spicy. Consider this a well-made "barley schnapps."

THE LAST DROP

Scotland

www.lastdropdistillers.com

This unusual super-premium blend is the brainchild of three industry veterans—Tom Jago, James Espey, and Peter Fleck. Allegedly, a random discovery of very old whiskies pre-vatted at 12 years of age and then allowed to mature for a further 36 years in sherry casks, The Last Drop would appear to have been something of an accident and cannot be repeated. Included in the blend are whiskies from long-lost distilleries, the youngest reputed to have been distilled in 1960. Savor the tasting notes—at £1,000 or so a bottle, and with only 1,347 bottles available, it may be the closest you'll get to tasting it.

THE LAST DROP ▶

BLEND 54.5% ABV

Exceptionally complex nose, with figs, chocolate, and vanilla. An unusual combination of new-mown hay, dried fruit, herbs, and butter cookies.

LAUDER'S

Scotland

Owner: MacDuff International

Between 1886 and 1893, Lauder's Royal Northern Cream scooped up a total of six gold medals in international competitions—a tribute to the meticulous research and repeated trials undertaken by the original proprietor, Archibald Lauder, a Glasgow publican. The development of the blend is said to have taken him two years. Today Lauder's is once again blended in Glasgow, by MacDuff International, and Lauder's Bar on Sauchiehall Street remains to commemorate Lauder himself. His blend has largely slipped from public view in its homeland, but is imported by Barton Brands of Chicago to the US, where it remains popular among value-conscious consumers.

◀ **LAUDER'S**

BLEND 40% ABV

A light and fruity blend designed for session drinking and mixing.

LEDAIG

Scotland

Tobermory Distillery,
Tobermory, Isle of Mull

Tobermory, the capital of Mull and the island's main port, was originally called Ledaig, and this was the name chosen by John Sinclair when he began distilling here in 1798. Quite when the Ledaig Distillery became Tobermory is unclear, as it has had an incredibly interrupted life, spending more time in mothballs than in production. In recent years the distillery adopted a similar approach to Springbank, producing a heavily peated robust West Coast malt called Ledaig and a lightly peated malt called Tobermory. At present there is a 10-year-old Ledaig, first released in 2008, and a 10- and a 15-year-old Tobermory *(see p346)*.

LEDAIG 10-YEAR-OLD ▶
SINGLE MALT: ISLANDS
43% ABV
Slightly medicinal, but full of dry, slightly dusty peat smoke.

LIMEBURNERS

Australia

Great Southern Distilling Company,
252 Frenchman Bay Road, Albany,
Western Australia
www.distillery.com.au

The Great Southern Distillery was built in 2007, the brainchild of lawyer and accountant Cameron Syme. Its location was chosen for Albany's cool, wet winters and enough breeze to provide 75 percent of its energy needs by wind power. It is close to the Margaret River wineries, which supply the ingredients for schnapps and liqueur-making. Limeburners whiskey is offered in single barrel bottlings: the first, Barrel M2, launched in April 2008, won an award.

◀ **LIMEBURNERS BARREL M11**
SINGLE MALT 43% ABV
The fourth bottling (M11), nicknamed "The Dark One," is from a French oak ex-brandy cask, re-racked into a second-fill ex-bourbon barrel.

LINKWOOD

Scotland
Elgin, Morayshire
www.malts.com

From the outset, Linkwood was a well-conceived distillery. It was surrounded by barley fields to supply the grain, and cattle to feed on the spent draff. The building you see today dates back to the 1870s, when the original Linkwood was demolished and a new distillery was built on the same site. It remained in private hands until 1933, when it became part of DCL.

LINKWOOD FLORA & FAUNA 12-YEAR-OLD ▶

SINGLE MALT: SPEYSIDE
43% ABV

On the lighter side of the Speyside style, with a fresh, grassy, green-apple fragrance and faint notes of spice. In the mouth it has a delicate sweet-and-sour flavor and a slow finish.

LINKWOOD RARE MALTS 26-YEAR-OLD

SINGLE MALT: SPEYSIDE
56.1% ABV

Bright and breezy for a 26-year-old. Lightly smoky with caramelized sugar notes. Spicy and warm in the finish.

LOCH FYNE

Scotland

Owner: Richard Joynson
www.lfw.co.uk

Created by Professor Ronnie Martin, a former production director at United Distillers (now Diageo), Loch Fyne is the exclusive and eponymous house blend of Loch Fyne Whiskies of Inverary. It is blended and bottled under license for this famous Scottish whisky specialist.

Slightly sweet and smoky, Loch Fyne is an easy-drinking, well-flavored blend, which has been praised by leading critics and won awards in international competition. Also available is a full-strength 12-year-old liqueur.

◄ LOCH FYNE PREMIUM SCOTCH
BLEND 40% ABV

Apple dumplings on the nose, enlivened by orange and tangerine notes. Subtle, with nutty, oil-related aromas and hints of smoke. The palate is smooth and well-balanced: acidic, salty, sweet, and dry. The finish is surprisingly warming.

LOCH LOMOND

Scotland
Alexandria, Dumbartonshire
www.lochlomonddistillery.com

Within the confines of the Loch Lomond Distillery, on the southern end of Loch Lomond, all manner of Scotch whiskies are produced, although originally it was just malt. The distillery was built in 1965 as a joint venture between Barton Brands of the US and Duncan Thomas. Twenty years later it was bought by Alexander Bulloch and his company, Glen Catrine Bonded Warehouse, Ltd. Today, grain whisky is produced alongside the malt. The distillery's stills have rectifying columns that can be adjusted to produce a lighter or heavier spirit.

LOCH LOMOND ▶
SINGLE MALT: HIGHLANDS
40% ABV
With no age statement and a competitive price, this is likely to be a fairly young single malt. It has a light, fresh flavor and no great influence of wood.

LOCHRANZA

Scotland
Isle of Arran Distillers, Lochranza, Isle of Arran
www.arranwhisky.com

This blended whisky is named after the picturesque village where the Isle of Arran Distillery is based. This was established as recently as 1995 by industry veteran Harold Currie, but has subsequently changed hands. Lochranza is a pleasant, easy-drinking standard blend. It may well see further development in future years as a proportion of the distillery's own mature stock of single malts can find its way into the recipe. Arran Distillers also produce the Robert Burns blend *(see p301)*.

◀ LOCHRANZA
BLEND 40% ABV
The initial impression is of melted toffee, followed by pears, oak, and hints of lime. Smooth and sweet, lightly sherried and oaky, with a medium finish. A dash of water helps the flavors.

LOCKE'S

Ireland

Cooley Distillery, Riverstown, Cooley, County Louth
www.cooleywhiskey.com

It's hard to believe that, just 30 years ago, this amazing distillery was almost derelict. Since the early 1950s, when the Locke's whiskey business first folded, the abandoned distillery buildings had been used to house pigs and farm machinery. Then, in the late 1970s, the local community got together and restored the distillery. After the renovation was completed, a deal was made with Cooley and, after decades of dusty silence, whiskey barrels once more appeared in the warehouses.

LOCKE'S 8-YEAR-OLD MALT ▶

SINGLE MALT 40% ABV

A vatting of Cooley's unpeated malt, with a top dressing of peated malt. It is not a bad whiskey; just a bit dull.

LOCKE'S BLEND

BLEND 40% ABV

This is a pleasant enough dram. It would be particularly good in a hot whiskey, where its limited range doesn't have to sing out.

LONG JOHN

Scotland
Owner: Chivas Brothers

Despite reasonably healthy sales in France, Scandinavia, and some Spanish-speaking markets, Long John appears very much the poor relation in the Chivas Brothers' stable, dominated as it is by Chivas Regal and Ballantine's. The brand has passed through a number of owners since it was founded in the early 19th century by the eponymous "Long" John MacDonald. The Scottish Whisky Association's Directory of Member's Brands lists a non-age version as well as a 12- and 15-year-old.

◀ LONG JOHN 12-YEAR-OLD
BLEND 40% ABV
The blend is said to contain 48 different malts, including Laphroaig and Highland Park. A deluxe blend, Long John 12-year-old is a dark, traditional style of whisky, noted for its distinctive character.

LONGMORN

Scotland
Elgin, Morayshire

John Duff, George Thomson and Charles Shirres went into partnership in 1894 and built the Longmorn distillery. With its four stills, it was conceived on a grand scale at a cost of £20,000 (around £2m in today's money). Within five years Duff had bought out his partners and built another distillery, BenRiach, next door.

Since 2000, 15-year-old bottling has been replaced by one a year older, clearly aimed at the super-premium category of malts.

LONGMORN 16-YEAR-OLD ▶
SINGLE MALT: SPEYSIDE
48% ABV

Its cereal aroma is sweetened with coconut from aging in bourbon casks. The mouthfeel is smooth and silky and dries on the tongue to give a crisp, slightly austere finish.

LONGMORN CASK STRENGTH 17-YEAR-OLD 1991
SINGLE MALT: SPEYSIDE
49.4% ABV

Richly floral on the nose and palate. Vanilla and ripe pears combine beautifully with tantalizing oaky notes.

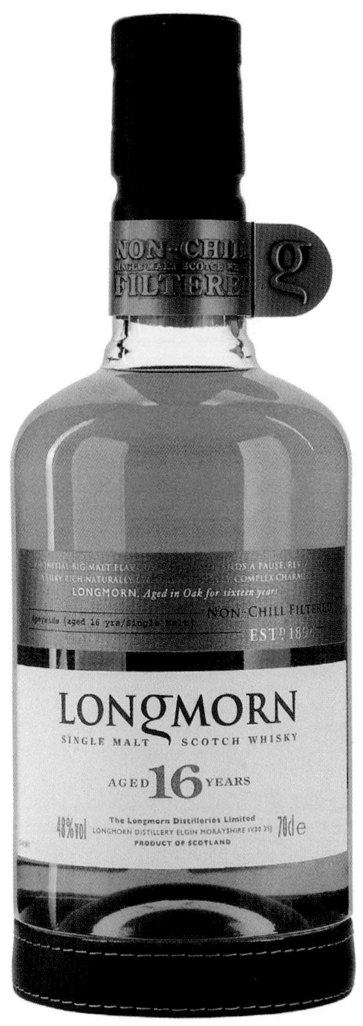

LONGROW

Scotland

Springbank Distillery,
Well Close, Campbeltown, Argyll
www.springbankdistillers.com

In 1973, the Springbank Distillery decided to distill a pungent, heavily smoked whisky alongside its main malt. The new whisky was christened Longrow after a distillery that had once stood next door. It was released as an experiment in 1985 and finally became a regular fixture in 1992.

Today, the core range includes the 10-year-old, its cask strength sibling—the 10-year-old 100 Proof—and the 14-year-old.

◀ LONGROW 10-YEAR-OLD

SINGLE MALT: CAMPBELTOWN
46% ABV

This dense, phenolic whisky has plenty of smoky complexity, alongside some sweetness from maturing in a mix of ex-bourbon and sherry casks.

LONGROW 14-YEAR-OLD

SINGLE MALT: CAMPBELTOWN
46% ABV

Coal smoke on the nose and coal dust on the palate—to phenol-lovers this is manna. An industrial-tasting mix of hot tar, brine, and coke.

MACALLAN

Scotland
Easter Elchies, Craigellachie, Morayshire
www.themacallan.com

The Macallan was first licensed in 1824 as the Elchies Distillery. It was a small operation: annual production at Macallan was just 40,000 gallons (180,000 liters) when it was sold to Roderick Kemp in 1892. The distillery was expanded and stayed in family control until 1996, when it was bought by Highland Distillers (now part of the Edrington Group), for £180 million. ☛

THE MACALLAN 10-YEAR-OLD ▶
SINGLE MALT: SPEYSIDE
40% ABV
The signature Macallan, matured in sherry butts. This popular whisky has a dried-fruit, slightly toffee-scented nose and a well-rounded flavor.

THE MACALLAN FINE OAK 10-YEAR-OLD
SINGLE MALT: SPEYSIDE
40% ABV
With less sherry influence, more of the fresh, brisk, malty distillery character comes through.

MACALLAN

In the intervening years, the distillery was rebuilt in the 1950s and the number of stills grew to 21. More importantly, The Macallan 10-year-old established itself as one of the leading single malts on Speyside. The distillery had always used sherry casks, which were shipped in from Spain. A deep amber color and fruitcake character came to symbolize the whisky. So the launch of the Fine Oak series in 2004, which uses bourbon casks alongside sherry butts, marked a radical departure. It has clearly widened The Macallan's appeal, however.

◀ THE MACALLAN 30-YEAR-OLD

SINGLE MALT: SPEYSIDE
43% ABV

A big, post-prandial malt with a sweet, sherried nose and spicy flavors of orange peel, cloves, and dates that linger on the finish.

THE MACALLAN 25-YEAR-OLD

SINGLE MALT: SPEYSIDE
43% ABV

Spicy citrus notes accompany the ripe dried-fruit character from the sherry casks, which lead to a little wood- smoke on the tongue.

MACARTHUR'S

Scotland

Owner: Inver House Distillers

The MacArthur clan of Argyllshire fought nobly alongside Robert the Bruce in the struggle for Scottish independence and subsequently gave their name to this standard blend. Like so many others, it has its roots in the upsurge of blending from independent merchants in the late-Victorian era and can be traced to the 1870s. Today it is owned by Inver House Distillers, who describe it as having a "light, smooth flavor with toffee and vanilla from cask aging." MacArthur's is not to be confused with single malts bottled independently under the label James MacArthur.

MACARTHUR'S ▶
BLEND 40% ABV
Fragrant, barley-malt nose with sweet, citrus aftertones. A medium-bodied, uncomplicated whisky, softly aromatic, with a smooth, mellow palate and a fresh, lingering finish.

MACKMYRA

Sweden

Mackmyra, Bruksgatan 4,
81832 Valbo
www.mackmyra.se

Founded in 1999, Mackmyra launched Preludium 01, the first bottling in a limited series, in 2006. Preludiums 02, 03, 04, and 05 followed in rapid succession. Preludium 06 was released in December 2007, followed by Special 01 in June 2008. The distillery also offers single cask Reserve bottlings.

◀ MACKMYRA PRELUDIUM 06
SINGLE MALT 50.5% ABV
Fruity, with aromas of lemon, pear, banana, and honey. Gentle hints of caramel, roast oak, and pepper. A distinctive smoky character, with undertones of juniper. The finish brings sweetness, charred oak cask, smoke, and a touch of salt.

MACKMYRA PRELUDIUM 05
SINGLE MALT 48.4% ABV
Marzipan, custard, and a light citrus note on the nose. Flavors of crème brûlée, bitter chocolate, and lemon zest. A bit oily; slightly metallic and grainy in the finish—creamier when mixed with water.

MAGILLIGAN

Ireland

Cooley Distillery, Riverstown, Cooley, County Louth

This is a confusing whiskey. It may well say pure pot still on the label, but you are actually buying a young, Cooley-produced single malt (though the Magilligan brand is not part of Cooley's own stable). The fault lies with Irish legislature; it has not legally defined what constitutes a "pure pot still." At the moment, any whiskey that is made in a pot still can be called pot still whiskey. So, buyers should beware.

Magilligan comes in various guises, including a limited-edition 1991 vintage bottled at 46% ABV.

MAGILLIGAN ▶
SINGLE MALT 43% ABV
This is a thin young malt, with hints of greatness, but it has been bottled as an adolescent. An 8-year-old version is available, but the regular Magilligan offering tastes like a vatting of whiskeys between three and five years old.

MAKER'S MARK

USA

3350 Burks Springs Road,
Loretto, Kentucky
www.makersmark.com

Maker's Mark Distillery is located on the banks of Hardin's Creek, near Loretto. Established in 1805, it is the USA's oldest working distillery remaining on its original site. The Maker's Mark brand was developed during the 1950s by Bill Samuels, Jr., and is now owned by Fortune Brands, Inc.

◄ MAKER'S MARK

BOURBON 45% ABV

A subtle, complex, and clean nose, with vanilla and spice, a delicate floral note of roses, plus lime and cocoa beans. Medium in body, it offers a palate of fresh fruit, spices, eucalyptus, and ginger cake. The finish features more spices, fresh oak with a hint of smoke, and a final flash of peach cheesecake.

MANNOCHMORE

Scotland
Elgin, Morayshire
www.malts.com

From conception, Mannochmore's simple role in life was supplying malt for Haig, then the top-selling blend in the UK. Fourteen years later it fell victim to the over-supply in the industry and was mothballed, as the big distillers sought to drain the whisky loch. It was back in production by 1989 and launched its first official malt as part of the Flora & Fauna range three years later.

MANNOCHMORE FLORA & FAUNA 12-YEAR-OLD ▶

SINGLE MALT: SPEYSIDE
43% ABV

An aperitif-style malt, with a light, floral nose but, in the mouth, a more luscious, spicy character, with hints of licorice and vanilla, comes through.

MANNOCHMORE RARE MALTS 22-YEAR-OLD

SINGLE MALT: SPEYSIDE
60.1% ABV

Distilled in 1974, this limited edition exudes fragrant, flowery aromas. Herbaceous and peppery, with a touch of peat in the mix.

MASTERSTROKE

India

Owner: Diageo Radico
www.radicokhaitan.com
www.diageo.com

Masterstroke De Luxe Whiskey, an IMFL (Indian Made Foreign Liquor) priced for the "prestige" category, was launched by Diageo Radico in February 2007. The company is a joint 50:50 venture between Radico Khaitan, Ltd., "India's fastest-growing liquor manufacturer," and the world's largest drinks company, Diageo. It is their first joint venture. Within three months the brand was being endorsed by Bollywood superstar Shah Rukh Khan.

◀ **MASTERSTROKE**
BLEND 42.8% ABV
A rich nose and mouthfeel, lent by a liberal amount of Blair Athol single malt. Well-balanced, with the light finish characteristic of IMFLs.

MCCARTHY'S

USA

Clear Creek Distillery,
2389 NW Wilson Street,
Portland, Oregon
www.clearcreekdistillery.com

Steve McCarthy established Clear Creek Distillery more than 20 years ago and has been distilling whiskey for over a decade. He is of the opinion that, since it is made from peat-malted barley brought in from Scotland, "our whiskey would be a single malt Scotch if Oregon were Scotland."

MCCARTHY'S OREGON ▶
SINGLE MALT 40% ABV

McCarthy's is initially matured in former sherry casks for two or three years, then for six to twelve months in barrels made from air-dried Oregon oak. Kippery and spicy on the nose, with a hint of sulfur, peat, and vanilla. It is big-bodied and oily, smoky-sweet on the meaty palate, and with dry oak, malt, spice, and salt in the long finish.

MCCLELLAND'S

Scotland
Owner: Morrison Bowmore

The range of McClelland's single malts offers a chance to explore Scotland and four of its key whisky-distilling regions. It was first launched in 1986, with a Highland, Lowland, and Islay expression. These proved so successful that a Speyside expression was introduced in 1999. According to the company, each one is carefully selected to reflect the true essence and

◄ MCCLELLAND'S HIGHLAND
SINGLE MALT: HIGHLANDS 40% ABV
Delicate wood notes on the nose, with sweet buttercream and fresh vanilla.Some initial sweetness, giving way to fresh fruit and lime hints.

MCCLELLAND'S ISLAY
SINGLE MALT: ISLAY 40% ABV
The nose is unmistakably Islay: wood smoke and cinders, tar, vanilla, and citrus hints. Forceful sea salt, burnt oak, and peat smoke, with vanilla undertones on the palate.

character of the region in which it is produced.

The brand currently claims to be number four in the US market, where it competes against Glenlivet, Glenfiddich, and The Macallan. It is also distributed to global markets, including Taiwan, Austria, South Africa, Japan, Canada, France, Russia, and the Netherlands. A Speyside 12-year-old was launched in November 2008 and will be joined by Highland, Lowland, and Islay 12-year-olds.

MCCLELLAND'S LOWLAND ▶
SINGLE MALT: LOWLANDS
40% ABV
A richly floral nose with hints of nutmeg, ginger, and citrus fruits. Very clean and delicate on the palate, with floral notes.

MCCLELLAND'S SPEYSIDE
SINGLE MALT: SPEYSIDE
40% ABV
Fresh mint, cut pine, hints of dark chocolate, and sweet malt on the nose. Initially sweet, developing nutty flavors and floral hints.

MCDOWELL'S

India

Owner: United Spirits
www.unitedspirits.in

Scotsman Angus McDowell founded McDowell & Co. in Madras in 1826 as a trading company specializing in liquor and cigars. McDowell's No.1 was launched in 1968.

A malt whiskey distillery was commissioned by McDowell & Co. at Ponda, Goa, in 1971. The spirit is matured in ex-bourbon casks for around three years. It is claimed that the heat and humidity of Goa leads to a more rapid maturation.

The product is described as "the first-ever indigenously developed single malt whiskey in Asia."

◀ MCDOWELL'S NO.1 RESERVE

BLEND 42.8% ABV

"Blended with Scotch and Select Indian Malts," this has a nose of dried figs and sweet tobacco and, later, prunes and dates. A sweet taste initially, then burned sugar and a short finish.

MCDOWELL'S SINGLE MALT

SINGLE MALT 42.8% ABV

With fresh cereal and fruit on the nose and a sweet, pleasantly citric taste, this is not unlike a young Speyside.

MELLOW CORN

USA

Heaven Hill Distillery,
1701 West Breckinridge Street,
Louisville, Kentucky
www.heaven-hill.com

According to Heaven Hill, "The forerunner and kissing cousin to Bourbon, American straight corn whiskey is defined by the US Government as having a recipe or mashbill with a minimum of 81 percent corn, the rest being malted barley and rye."

Today, Heaven Hill is the sole remaining national producer of this classic whiskey style, bottling Georgia Moon *(see p128)* in addition to Mellow Corn.

MELLOW CORN ▶

CORN WHISKEY 50% ABV

Wood varnish and vanilla, with floral and herbal notes on the nose. The palate is big, oily, and fruity, with candy apples. More fruit, toffee, and understated vanilla complete the finish. Young and boisterous.

MICHAEL COLLINS

Ireland
www.michaelcollinswhiskey.com

Despite the fame of General Michael Collins among the Irish people, most of them have never heard of this whiskey.

The reason for this is that it was initially formulated for the American market by Cooley Distillery in conjunction with US importer Sidney Frank. However, it can now be bought on both sides of the Atlantic.

Unusually for an Irish whiskey, the Michael Collins malt is double-distilled and lightly peated. The blend is a mix of the malt and a younger grain whiskey.

◀ MICHAEL COLLINS SINGLE MALT
SINGLE MALT 40% ABV
Soft and drinkable, with plenty of biscuity flavors. Vanilla notes emerge, with a hint of light smoke.

MICHAEL COLLINS BLEND
BLEND 40% ABV
Less impressive than the malt. It is thin, with the scent of woody embers at its core, but it lacks a decent finish.

MIDLETON

Ireland
Midleton, County Cork
www.irishdistillers.ie

Among all the spirits produced at Midleton—Jameson, Powers, Paddy, and all of the Irish Distillers' portfolio of whiskeys—there is just one regularly appearing whiskey that carries the actual Midleton moniker. Launched in 1984, Midleton Very Rare is for the premium market and the price reflects whatever that market can bear. A new vintage is released late every year.

MIDLETON VERY RARE ▶
BLEND 40% ABV
On the nose, classy oak and bold cereal notes dance on a high wire made of pure beeswax. The body is full and yielding, and the finish breaks on the tongue in waves of silky, walnut whip.

MIDLETON MASTER DISTILLER'S PRIVATE COLLECTION 1973
PURE POT STILL 56% ABV
A bottling of pure pot still whiskey from the old Midleton Distillery. Just 800 bottles were released. Its taste is said to be spicy, fruity, and honeyed, with some dry, sherry nuttiness.

MILFORD

New Zealand
The New Zealand Malt Whisky Company & Preston Associates, 14–16 Harbour St., Oamaru
www.milfordwhisky.co.nz

Milford whiskey was originally made at Willowbank Distillery in Dunedin, South Island, which was owned by the Wilson Brewery *(see Lammerlaw, p224)*. The New Zealand Malt Whisky Company now owns the Milford label (and also the less prestigious Prestons label) and is building a new distillery at Bannockburn, Central Otago. It has also opened a retail warehouse at Oamaru, where the new Milford malt will be matured and bottled.

◄ **MILFORD 10-YEAR-OLD**
SINGLE MALT 43% ABV
Often compared to a Scottish Lowland malt, Milford's 10-year-old has a light, dry, and fragrant nose; the taste is sweet, then dry, with a slightly woody, short finish.

MILLARS

Ireland

Cooley Distillery, Riverstown,
Cooley, County Louth
www.cooleywhiskey.com

Once upon a time, every single drop of Irish whiskey was bottled by bonders. Gilbey's, Mitchell's, or Millars would buy whiskey in bulk and sell it to their customers, often straight from the cask. This method started to die out during the latter part of the 20th century, and Adam Millars & Co in Dublin was one of the only bonders to survive.

The Millars brand is now owned by Cooley, and this hard-to-find whiskey is a grain-heavy blend.

MILLARS SPECIAL RESERVE ▶

BLEND 40% ABV

This is a superb little whiskey. It is a perky dram, with a real sense of fun. A peppery character on the nose is underpinned by a luxurious, spicy body in the glass.

MILLBURN

Scotland
Inverness, Inverness-shire

It was Millburn's misfortune to be located on the outskirts of Inverness on the road to Elgin. When the whisky industry suffered one of its big periodic downturns in the 1980s, the distillery was in the wrong place at the wrong time—not remote enough to simply be mothballed when there was the prospect of redevelopment instead. And so it shut down for good in 1985 and was turned into a steakhouse. Today, it's a hotel and restaurant called The Auld Distillery. Limited-edition bottlings are still released intermittently by the owner of its stocks, Diageo.

◀ MILLBURN RARE MALTS 25-YEAR-OLD
SINGLE MALT: SPEYSIDE
61.9% ABV

This Rare Malts bottling is a big, meaty whisky that is dry and chewy in the mouth, with damp wood, smoke, and orange skins.

MILLSTONE

The Netherlands
Zuidam, Weverstraat 6, 5111 PW, Baarle Nassau
www.zuidam-distillers.com

What started as a gin distillery some 50 years ago is now a company with a second generation of the Zuidam family at the helm. It produces beautifully crafted single malts, alongside excellent young and old *jenevers*, as the Dutch call their gin. The Millstone 5-year-old single malt whiskey was introduced in 2007, to be followed by an 8-year-old sibling. Zuidam uses ex-bourbon as well as ex-sherry casks to mature its whiskey. A 10-year-old expression is in the making.

MILLSTONE 5-YEAR-OLD ▶
SINGLE MALT 40% ABV
Delicate aromas of fruit and honey combined with vanilla, wood, and a hint of coconut. Rich honey sweetness in the mouth, delicate spicy notes, and a long vanilla-oak finish.

MILTONDUFF

Scotland
Miltonduff, Elgin, Morayshire

Once one of the illicit stills that were rife in Speyside in the 19th century, Miltonduff has been owned by Pernod Ricard since 2005. Much of the 1.2 million gallon (5.5 million liter) output is used to supply malt for its top-selling blend, Ballantine's Finest. An official 15-year-old malt is now available, although a wider range of bottlings exists among the independents, particularly Gordon & MacPhail.

◄ MILTONDUFF 15-YEAR-OLD

SINGLE MALT: SPEYSIDE
46% ABV

This non chill-filtered distillery bottling is hard to find. It has a gentle Speyside character with a honeyed, leathery aroma and a nutty, herbal flavor.

MILTONDUFF GORDON & MACPHAIL 1968

SINGLE MALT: SPEYSIDE
40% ABV

This rare Gordon & MacPhail bottling has a rich sherried character with notes of licorice, menthol, and crystallized ginger.

MONKEY SHOULDER

Scotland

Owner: William Grant & Sons

The name may seem contrived, but this blended malt from William Grant & Sons refers to a condition known among workers in the maltings—turning the damp grain by hand, they often incurred a repetitive strain injury.

Three metal monkeys decorate the shoulder of the bottle and just three single malts go into the blend—Glenfiddich, Balvenie, and Kininvie. At the launch, great play was made of the whisky's mixability, and you're as likely to encounter it on a cocktail menu as you are in your local liquor store.

MONKEY SHOULDER ▶

BLEND 40% ABV

Banana, honey, pears, and allspice on the nose. Vanilla, nutmeg, citrus hints, and generic fruit on the palate. A dry finish, then a short burst of menthol.

MORTLACH

Scotland
Dufftown, Keith, Banffshire
www.malts.com

The six stills at Mortlach are configured in a uniquely complex manner, with a fifth of the spirit being triple-distilled in an intermediate still called "Wee Witchie." This process is intended to add richness and depth to the spirit, which is then condensed in traditional worm tubs outdoors, to create a more robust style of whisky.

◀ MORTLACH FLORA & FAUNA 16-YEAR-OLD

SINGLE MALT: SPEYSIDE
43% ABV

As suggested by the rich amber color, there is a strong sherry influence at play, although not enough to unbalance this beguiling, complex malt with notes of dark mint-chocolate on the nose.

MORTLACH 21-YEAR-OLD

SINGLE MALT: SPEYSIDE
43% ABV

Caramel and soft fruits on the nose. The palate is drier, with the sherry wood influence bringing resinous, oaky flavors.

MURREE

Pakistan
Murree Distillery, National Park Road, Rawalpindi
www.murreebrewery.com

With a dispensation having been granted to the non-Muslim owners of Murree to distill alcoholic drinks "for visitors and non-Muslims," this is the only distillery of alcoholic beverages in a Muslim country.

The barley comes from the UK and is malted in floor maltings and Saladin boxes. Some of the spirit is filled into cask, most into large vats (some made from Australian oak), and matured in cellars equipped with a cooling system.

MURREE'S CLASSIC 8-YEAR-OLD ▶
SINGLE MALT 43% ABV
A flowery nose and finish, somewhat green, with a hard candy taste. Unlikely to be pure malt whiskey.

MURREE'S RAREST 21-YEAR-OLD
SINGLE MALT 43% ABV
This is the oldest whiskey to have been produced in Asia. The Murree key notes have developed and deepened with a big dose of wood-extractive flavors.

NANT

Australia

The Nant Estate, Bothwell, Tasmania
www.nantdistillery.com.au

The Nant estate in Tasmania, founded in 1821, was bought by Keith and Margaret Batt in 2004 with a view to building a distillery on the historic working farm. With the expert guidance of Bill Lark *(see p228)*, the distillery went into production in April 2008. The plan is to produce a limited number of casks each year. The barley and water for the distillery come from the estate, while a restored mill provides the grist. There is also an elegant new visitor center.

◀ **NANT DOUBLE MALT**
BLENDED MALT 43% ABV
This is a vatting of two casks selected from other Tasmanian distilleries, and gives an idea of what Nant's own whiskey will taste like. Sweet and fruity, with plums and cream soda, it is medium-bodied and smooth.

NIKKA—GRAIN & BLENDS

Japan
Nikka 1, Aobaku, Sendaishi, Miyagiken; Kurokawacho 7–6, Yoichimachi, Yoichigun, Hokkaido
www.nikka.com

Japan's second-largest distillery company was founded in 1933 by Masataka Taketsuru. This charismatic distiller had learned whiskey-making in Scotland—at Longmorn on Speyside and at Hazelburn in Campbeltown. ☛

NIKKA WHISKEY FROM THE BARREL ▶

BLEND 51.4% ABV

Nikka's award-winning blend of malts and grain is given further aging in first-fill bourbon casks. The nose is upfront, and slightly floral, with good intensity, peachiness, and a lift akin to rosemary oil and pine sap. The palate is lightly sweet, with some vanilla, a hint of cherry, and plenty of spiciness on the finish. This is a top blend.

NIKKA ALL MALT

BLENDED MALT 40% ABV

A blend of pot still malt and 100 percent malt from a Coffey still. Sweet, dry oak on the nose alongside banana. The palate is soft and unctuous.

NIKKA—GRAIN & BLENDS

His company, Nikka, operates two malt distilleries at Yoichi and Miyagikyo. It also has grain plants and a growing portfolio of styles, including blends and single malts.

Recently, Nikka has been focusing on the export market. Although its blends are available overseas, its commercial push has been through its single-malt range branded as Nikka Miyagikyo and Nikka Yoichi.

◀ NIKKA PURE MALT RED

BLENDED MALT 43% ABV

Nikka produces a blended malt range called the Pure Malt Series. The Red is light and fragrant, with faint hints of pineapple, fresh apple, pear, and a gentle almondlike oakiness.

NIKKA SINGLE COFFEY MALT

MALTED BARLEY MASH 55% ABV

This unusual whiskey is made by distilling a 100 percent malted-barley mash in a Coffey still. As a result, no one is sure if it is a malt or a grain. The nose is gentle, sweet, and rounded, with notes of banana, honey, coconut, persimmon, and dry grass. On the palate it is chewy and sweet, with nutmeg, cinnamon, peach, and vanilla.

NIKKA MIYAGIKYO

Japan
Nikka 1, Aobaku, Sendaishi, Miyagiken
www.nikka.com

Also known as Sendai after its nearest town, Miyagikyo was the second distillery built by Nikka. Today, it has a malt distillery with eight stills, a grain plant with two different set-ups, and extensive warehousing. The predominant style is lightly fragrant and softly fruity, but there are some peaty examples, too.

NIKKA MIYAGIKYO 10-YEAR-OLD ▶

SINGLE MALT 45% ABV

Typical of the main distillery character, this has an attractive floral lift (lilies, hot gorse, lilac), with a touch of anise in the background. The palate shows balanced, crisp oak, some butterscotch notes, and a pinelike finish.

NIKKA MIYAGIKYO

SINGLE MALT 45% ABV

The extra two years fill out the nose with flowers, giving way to soft tropical fruits, such as mango and persimmon, as well as a richer vanilla pod character. Good structure, with a wisp of smoke.

NIKKA TAKETSURU

Japan
Nikka 1, Aobaku, Sendaishi, Miyagiken; Kurokawacho 7–6, Yoichimachi, Yoichigun, Hokkaido
www.nikka.com

This small range of blended (vatted) malts is named after the founder of Nikka, Masataka Taketsuru. Like the Pure Malt Series, it is made up of component whiskeys from the firm's two sites.

◄ NIKKA TAKETSURU 17-YEAR-OLD

BLENDED MALT 43% ABV

There's obvious smoke at work here: some cigar-box aromas, varnish, and light leather. When diluted, a fresh tropical-fruit character comes out. This is what leads on the palate, before the peat smoke begins to assert itself.

NIKKA TAKETSURU 21-YEAR-OLD

BLENDED MALT 43% ABV

With this multi-award winner, the smoke is immediate while the spirit behind is thicker, richer, and darker: ripe berries, cake mix, oak, and a touch of mushroom or truffle indicative of age. Fruit syrups, figs, prunes, and smoke.

NIKKA YOICHI

Japan
Kurokawacho 7–6, Yoichimachi,
Yoichigun, Hokkaido
www.nikka.com

Although Yoichi's malts are most definitely Japanese, they do have close resemblances to their cousins in Scotland—the whiskies of Islay and Campbeltown in particular. A wide range of styles is made, but Yoichi is famous for its complex, robust, oily, and smoky malts.

NIKKA YOICHI 10-YEAR-OLD ▶
SINGLE MALT 45% ABV
There's a hint of maltiness in here. Salt spray and light smoke on the nose initially, with some caramelized fruit notes. Yoichi's oiliness coats the tongue while the smoke changes from fragrant to sooty with dried flowers in the finish.

NIKKA YOICHI 12-YEAR-OLD
SINGLE MALT 45% ABV
This is classic Yoichi—big, deep, robust, and complex. The peatiness adds an earthy character to the coal-like sootiness. Poached pear and baked peach give a balancing sweetness, offset by smoke, licorice, and heather.

THE NOTCH

USA

Triple Eight Distillery,
5&7 Bartlett Farm Road,
Nantucket, Massachusetts
www.ciscobrewers.com

Dean and Melissa Long started up their Nantucket Winery in 1981, and added the Cisco Brewery in 1995. Two years later they founded the region's only micro-distillery, Triple Eight. The first single malt whiskey was distilled in 2000 and is called The Notch Whiskey, because it is "not Scotch," though it is produced in the Scottish style. It is matured in former bourbon barrels before being finished in French oak Merlot barrels.

◀ THE NOTCH

SINGLE MALT 44.4% ABV

Sweet aromas of almonds and fruit on the nose, backed by vanilla and toasted oak. Mellow honey and pear notes are present on the palate, which also contains a suggestion of Merlot. The finish is lengthy and herbal.

OBAN

Scotland
Oban, Argyll
www.malts.com

Oban Distillery dates back to 1793, when Oban itself was a tiny West Coast fishing village. Since then the town—which is dubbed "The Gateway to the Isles"—has grown up around it, preventing the distillery from growing.

Since 1988, Oban has been one of Diageo's "Classic Malts," albeit the smallest of them. Given the success of the range, its owners may wonder whether it should have picked a larger distillery.

OBAN 14-YEAR-OLD ▶
SINGLE MALT: HIGHLANDS
43% ABV
The brisk, maritime distillery character is mellowed by the years in wood. The influence of sherry adds a rich, dried-fruit character.

OBAN DISTILLERS EDITION 1992
SINGLE MALT: HIGHLANDS
43% ABV
A 15-year-old malt, aged in different casks during maturation. Spicy and oaky flavors dominate from the strong sherry-wood effect.

OLD CHARTER

USA

Buffalo Trace Distillery,
1001 Wilkinson Boulevard,
Frankfort, Kentucky
www.buffalotrace.com

The Old Charter brand dates back to 1874, and the name is a direct reference to the Charter Oak tree, where Connecticut's colonial charter was hidden from the English in 1687. The Buffalo Trace Distillery itself dates back to the early 1900s and is listed on the National Register of Historic Places.

◀ **OLD CHARTER 8-YEAR-OLD**
BOURBON 40% ABV

Initially dry and peppery on the nose, with sweet and buttery aromas following through. Mouth-coating, with fruit, vanilla, old leather, and cloves on the palate. The finish is long and sophisticated.

OLD CROW

USA

Jim Beam Distillery,
149 Happy Hollow Road,
Clermont, Kentucky
www.jimbeam.com

Old Crow takes its name from the 19th-century Scottish-born chemist and Kentucky distiller James Christopher Crow. Along with Old Grand-Dad and Old Taylor, this brand was acquired by Jim Beam from National Distillers in 1987, and the three distilleries associated with these bourbons were closed. All production now takes place at Jim Beam's distilleries in Boston and Clermont.

OLD CROW ▶

BOURBON 40% ABV

Complex on the nose, with malt, rye, and sharp fruit notes combining with gentle spice. The palate follows through with spicy, malty, and citric elements, with citrus and spice notes to the fore.

OLD FITZGERALD

USA

Heaven Hill Distillery,
1701 West Breckinridge Street,
Louisville, Kentucky
www.heaven-hill.com

Old Fitzgerald was named by John E. Fitzgerald, who founded a distillery at Frankfort in 1870. The brand moved to its present home of Louisville when the Stitzel brothers, Frederick and Philip, merged their company with that of William Larue Weller & Sons, and subsequently opened the new Stitzel-Weller distillery at Louisville in 1935.

◄ **VERY SPECIAL OLD FITZGERALD 12-YEAR-OLD**

BOURBON 45% ABV

A complex and well-balanced bourbon, made with some wheat in the mashbill, rather than rye. The nose is rich, fruity, and leathery, while the palate exhibits sweet and fruity notes balanced by spices and oak. The finish is long and drying, with vanilla fading to oak.

OLD FORESTER

USA

Brown-Forman Distillery,
850 Dixie Highway,
Louisville, Kentucky
www.brown-forman.com

The origins of the Old Forester brand date back to 1870, when George Garvin Brown established a distillery in Louisville, Kentucky. The whiskey initially used the spelling "Forrester," and some say the name was selected to honor Confederate army officer General Nathan Bedford Forrest.

OLD FORESTER ▶

BOURBON 43% ABV

Complex, with pronounced floral notes, vanilla, spice, pepper, fruit, chocolate, and menthol on the nose. Full and fruity in the mouth, where rye and peaches vie with fudge, nutmeg, and oak. The finish offers more rye, toffee, licorice, and drying oak.

OLD FORESTER BIRTHDAY BOURBON (2007)

BOURBON 47% ABV

The 2007 release is sweet on the nose, with cinnamon, caramel, vanilla, and mint. The palate is full and complex, with caramel, apples, and vanilla oak. The finish is lengthy, warm, and clean.

OLD GRAND-DAD

USA

Jim Beam Distillery,
149 Happy Hollow Road,
Clermont, Kentucky
www.jimbeam.com

Old Grand-Dad was established in 1882 by a grandson of distiller Basil Hayden *(see p39)*. The brand and its distillery eventually passed into the hands of American Brands (now Fortune Brands Inc.) which subsequently closed the distillery. Production now takes place in the Jim Beam distilleries in Clermont and Boston.

◀ OLD GRAND-DAD
BOURBON 43–57% ABV
Made with a comparatively high percentage of rye, the nose of Old Grand-Dad reveals oranges and peppery spices. Quite heavy-bodied, the taste is full, yet surprisingly smooth, considering the strength. Fruit, nuts, and caramel are foremost on the palate, while the finish is long and oily.

OLD PARR

Scotland

Owner: Diageo

The original "Old Parr," was one Thomas Parr, who lived from 1483 to 1635, making him 152 years old when he died. If that seems improbable, his tomb can be inspected in Poets' Corner, Westminster Abbey.

In 1871, Old Parr's name was borrowed by two famous blenders of their day, the Greenlees brothers, for their deluxe whisky. Now under the stewardship of industry giants Diageo, the brand has gone on to success in Japan, Venezuela, Mexico, and Colombia. By tradition, Cragganmore is the mainstay of the blend.

GRAND OLD PARR ▶ 12-YEAR-OLD

BLEND 43% ABV

Pronounced malt, raisin, and orange notes on the nose, with some apple and dried-fruit undertones, and perhaps a hint of peat. Forceful on the palate, with flavors of malt, raisin, burned caramel, and brown sugar.

OLD POTRERO

USA

Anchor Distilling Company,
1705 Marisposa Street,
San Francisco, California
www.anchorbrewing.com

Fritz Maytag is one of the pioneers of the American "micro-drinks" movement. In 1994 he added a small distillery to his brewery on San Francisco's Potrero Hill. Here, Maytag aims to "re-create the original whiskey of America," by making small batches of spirits in traditional, open pot stills, using 100 percent rye malt.

◄ OLD POTRERO

SINGLE MALT RYE 62.55% ABV

This 18th-century-style whiskey displays a floral, nutty nose, with vanilla and spice. Oily and smooth on the palate, with mint, honey, chocolate, and pepper in the lengthy finish.

OLD POTRERO RYE

RYE WHISKEY 45% ABV

Aged for three years in new, charred-oak barrels, this 19th-century-style whiskey boasts nuts, buttery vanilla, sweet oak, and pepper on the nose. Complex in the mouth, oily, sweet, and spicy, with caramel, oak, and spicy rye notes in the finish.

OLD PULTENEY

Scotland
Pulteney Distillery, Wick, Caithness
www.oldpulteney.com

Wick was a tiny village when the British Fisheries Society, under the directorship of Sir William Pulteney decided to turn it into a model fishing port in the 1790s. In 1826, with the trade in herring booming, local distiller James Henderson named his new distillery in his honor.

The solitary wash still comes with a giant ball, to increase reflux, and a truncated top, supposedly lopped off to fit the still room.

OLD PULTENEY 12-YEAR-OLD ▶

SINGLE MALT: HIGHLANDS
40% ABV

A brisk, salty, maritime malt with a woody sweetness from aging in bourbon casks.

OLD PULTENEY 17-YEAR-OLD

SINGLE MALT: HIGHLANDS
46% ABV

The 17-year-old is partly matured in sherry wood, to add fruity, butterscotch notes to the flavor. Medium-full body in the mouth, with a long finish.

OLD SMUGGLER

Scotland
Owner: Gruppo Campari

Reputedly, and appropriately, a big favorite during Prohibition, Old Smuggler was first developed by James and George Stodart in 1835. Although the firm is today largely forgotten, history records that it was the first to marry its whisky in sherry butts. The brand is now owned by Gruppo Campari, who acquired it along with its sister blend Braemar and the flagship Glen Grant Distillery from Pernod Ricard in 2006. It continues to hold a significant position in the US and Argentina, where it is the second-bestselling whisky, and is reported to be developing strong sales in Eastern Europe.

◀ **OLD SMUGGLER**
BLEND 40% ABV
Decent Scotch with no offensive overtones and some smoke hints. Blended for value, and for drinking with a mixer.

OLD TAYLOR

USA

Jim Beam Distillery,
149 Happy Hollow Road,
Clermont, Kentucky
www.jimbeam.com

Old Taylor was introduced by Edmund Haynes Taylor, Jr., who was associated at various times with three distilleries in the Frankfort area of Kentucky, including what is now Buffalo Trace *(see p66)*. He was the man responsible for the Bottled-in-Bond Act of 1897, which guaranteed a whiskey's quality—any bottle bearing an official government seal had to be 100 proof (50% ABV) and at least four years old. Old Taylor was bought by Fortune Brands in 1987.

OLD TAYLOR ▶
BOURBON 40% ABV
Light and orangey on the nose, with a hint of marzipan; sweet, honeyed, and slightly oaky on the palate.

P&M

France

Domaine Mavela, Brasserie Pietra, Route de La Marana, 20600 Furiani, Corsica
www.brasseriepietra.com

P&M is a fruitful cooperation between two companies on the Mediterranean island of Corsica. Founded as a brewery in 1996, Pietra produces the mash that is distilled at Mavela. The pure malt whiskey is aged in casks made of oak from the local forest. Other spirits produced at Mavela include P&M Blend and P&M Blend Supérieur. Cask type and age are not specified.

◀ P&M PURE MALT

MALT 42% ABV

This complex, aromatic whiskey has a subtle aroma of honey, apricot, and citrus fruit, and a rich flavor.

PADDY

Ireland

Midleton Distillery, Midleton, County Cork
www.irishdistillers.ie

There was a time when Irish whiskey was sold anonymously from casks in pubs. What whiskey a pub stocked was down to the owner and his relationship with the agent for the distillery.

Paddy Flaherty was an agent for the Cork Distillers Company of Midleton in the 1920s and 30s. You knew when he was in town, as he'd buy everyone drinks at the bar, and the whiskey he sold—the CDC's Old Irish Whiskey—became so synonymous with the man himself that it was simply known as Paddy's whiskey.

PADDY ▶

BLEND 40% ABV

This is a malty dram, which is both solid and well matured. It offers a satisfying, spicy, peppery kick.

PASSPORT

Scotland

Owner: Chivas Brothers

Passport was developed by Seagram and acquired by Pernod Ricard in 2002. Like many brands that are invisible in the UK, it enjoys conspicuous success elsewhere: Passport's main strongholds are the US, South Korea, Spain, and Brazil, where its fruity taste lends itself to being served on the rocks, in mixed drinks, and in cocktails. Packaged in a distinctive retro, rectangular green bottle, Passport is "a unique Scotch whisky, inspired by the revolution of 1960s Britain, with a young and vibrant personality." Such distinguished and famous malts as Glenlivet are found in the blend.

◄ **PASSPORT**
BLEND 40% ABV
A fruity taste and a deliciously creamy finish. It can be served straight or, more usually, mixed over ice. Medium-bodied, with a soft and mellow finish.

PENDERYN

Wales
Penderyn, near Aberdare
www.welsh-whisky.co.uk

Currently the only whiskey distillery in Wales, Penderyn was named "Microdistillery Whiskey of the Year" in 2008 by leading American whiskey magazine *Malt Advocate*. It is indeed micro, producing only one cask a day. After a slow start, the distillery is now acknowledged worldwide as makers of exquisite whiskeys.

Penderyn whiskey is matured in ex-bourbon casks, mainly from Buffalo Trace and Evan Williams. The contents are then re-casked into ex-Madeira barrels—hence the sweet taste. The label does not state a specific age.

PENDERYN AUR CYMRU ▶
SINGLE MALT 46% ABV
Zesty and fresh, this malt is prickly, fruity, and bitter-sweet.

PENDERYN PEATED
SINGLE MALT 46% ABV
Sweet, aromatic smoke followed by vanilla, green apples, and refreshing citrus notes.

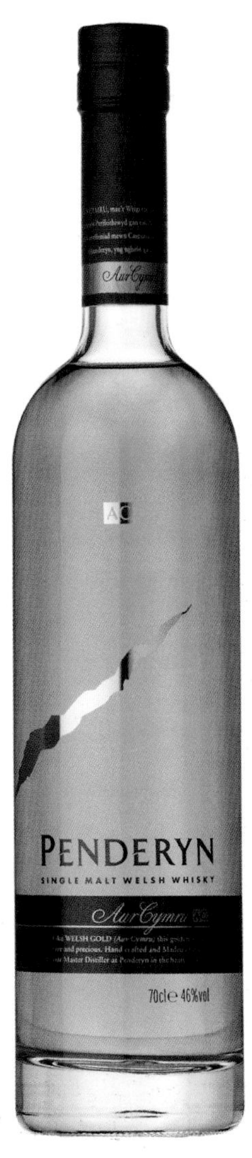

PEREGRINE ROCK

USA

Saint James Spirits,
5220 Fourth Street,
Irwindale, California
www.saintjamesspirits.com

Saint James Spirits was founded in 1995 by teacher Jim Busuttil, who learned the craft of distilling in Germany and Switzerland. He has been making single malt whisky (note the Scottish spelling) since 1997, and Peregrine Rock is produced from peated Scottish barley in a 40-US-gallon (150-liter) alambic copper pot still and put into bourbon barrels for a minimum period of three years.

◀ PEREGRINE ROCK CALIFORNIA PURE

SINGLE MALT 40% ABV

Floral on the nose, with fresh fruits and a hint of smoke. The palate is delicate and fruity, with a citric twist to it, while sweeter, malty, and new-mown-grass notes develop in the slightly smoky finish.

PIG'S NOSE

Scotland
Owner: Spencerfield Spirits
www.spencerfieldspirit.com

Should you visit one of the UK's many agricultural or county fairs, you may well encounter this whisky being sold from the back of an old horse box. Do not walk away: Pig's Nose has been re-blended by Whyte & Mackay's superstar master blender, Richard Paterson, and launched back on to the market in smart new livery. Brother to the better-known blended malt Sheep Dip *(see p315)*, Pig's Nose is a full-flavored and drinkable blend that more than lives up to the claim that "our Scotch is as soft and smooth as a pig's nose."

PIG'S NOSE ▶
BLEND 40% ABV
The nose is delicate and refined, with soft and sensual floral notes supported by complex fruit flavors. On the palate, there is a forceful array of malty flavors from Scotland's four distilling regions.

PIKESVILLE

USA

Heaven Hill Distillery,
1701 West Breckinridge Street,
Louisville, Kentucky
www.heaven-hill.com

Rye whiskeys fall into two stylistic types, namely the spicy, tangy Pennsylvania style, as exemplified by Rittenhouse *(see p300)*, and the Maryland style, which is softer in character. Pikesville is arguably the only example of Maryland rye still being produced today. This whiskey takes its name from Pikesville in Maryland, where it was first distilled during the 1890s and last produced in 1972. A decade later the brand was acquired by Heaven Hill.

◀ **PIKESVILLE SUPREME**
RYE WHISKEY 40% ABV
The crisp nose presents bubble gum, fruit, and wood varnish, while on the palate there is more bubble gum, spice, oak, and overt vanilla. The finish comprises lingering vanilla and oranges.

PINWINNIE ROYALE

Scotland
Owner: Inver House Distillers

Pinwinnie Royale stands out from the crowd, its label hinting at an early ecclesiastical manuscript and regal connections, though there is little to support these romantic suppositions. Given its place in the Inver House stable, it would seem likely that Old Pulteney, Speyburn, anCnoc, and Balblair single malts are to be found in the blend, with the emphasis on the lesser-known names. As well as the standard expression, there is a 12-year-old version, which mixes a light Speyside fruitiness with drier background wood notes, and a buttery texture.

PINWINNIE ROYALE ▶
BLEND 40% ABV
Young, spirity fruitiness on the nose, smooth-textured but spicy in the mouth, with burned, sooty notes in the finish.

POIT DHUBH

Scotland

Owner: The Gaelic Whisky Co.
www.gaelicwhisky.com

Pràban na Linne (known also as the Gaelic Whisky Co.) was established by Sir Iain Noble in 1976 to create employment in the south of Skye. The business has grown steadily since. Poit Dhubh (pronounced *Potch Ghoo*) is a non chill-filtered blended malt supplied as 8-, 12-, and 21-year-olds. A limited-edition 30-year-old was bottled for the company's 30th anniversary. Poit Dhubh makes much play of the possible bootleg nature of its whisky, stating, "We are unwilling either to confirm or deny that Poit Dhubh comes from an illicit still." This is, of course, complete fantasy.

◀ **POIT DHUBH 8-YEAR-OLD**
BLENDED MALT 43% ABV
Dried fruits and a light spiciness give a bittersweet character, with dry, woody notes and a trace of peat.

PORT ELLEN

Scotland

Port Ellen, Isle of Islay

Of all Islay malts, Port Ellen has possibly the largest cult following, owing to its rarity, which has increased every year since the distillery shut down in 1983. It was founded in 1825 by Alexander Kerr Mackay, and remained in family hands until the 1920s, when it became part of DCL (Distillers Company Ltd.). Its misfortune was to be part of the same stable as Lagavulin and Caol Ila: when the downturn came, it was the weakest link. Today it remains active as a maltings plant, supplying Islay's distilleries with most of their malt.

PORT ELLEN DOUGLAS LAING 26-YEAR-OLD ▶

SINGLE MALT: ISLAY 50% ABV

Matured in refill bourbon casks, this bottling has a sweet and fruity nose, with some new leather. Sweetness on the palate, but overwhelmed by peat smoke. A long, tarry finish, with a dab of salt.

POWERS

Ireland
Midleton Distillery, Midleton, County Cork
www.irishdistillers.ie

For longer than anyone could remember, Jameson and Powers used to stare each other down across the River Liffey in the heart of Dublin. The Powers family (on Dublin's south side) had been in the business since 1817, and a member of the family sat on the board of Irish Distillers until it was incorporated into the Pernod Ricard group, some 171 years later.

◀ POWERS GOLD LABEL

BLEND 40% ABV

This whiskey is something really special. The nose is classically Irish—at once bracing and brittle. At core, this whiskey is pure pot still, cut with just enough good grain. Powers Gold Label is an utterly captivating blend.

POWERS GOLD LABEL 12-YEAR-OLD

BLEND 40% ABV

An older, more layered expression of the same Powers formulation. Spice, honey, crème brûlée, with soft wood tones and sweet, fresh fruits.

PRIME BLUE

Scotland
Owner: Morrison Bowmore

Prime Blue is a blended malt available largely in Taiwan, where the market has developed in sensational style during the last decade. The color blue is said to convey nobility and royalty, and the brand name was reputedly chosen to reflect sophistication in the whisky's taste. At their peak, sales exceeded 1 million cases a year, although the market for this style in the Far East has declined somewhat in recent years and competition in Taiwan and elsewhere has intensified. Standard, 12-, 17-, and 21-year-old versions are available.

PRIME BLUE ▶
BLENDED MALT 40% ABV
Aromas of vanilla and malted barley are soon followed by light cocoa, and then heathery, floral notes. Initially fruity on the palate, followed by a malty sweetness, and a long finish.

GREAT WHISKEYS

P

PRINTER'S

Czech Republic

Stock Plzen, Palirenska 2,
32600 Plzen
www.stock.cz

Stock Plzen was founded in the 1920s and is the best-known spirits producer in the Czech Republic, with a high-profile, high-volume ethos. The company makes 40 different spirits, including Printer's Whiskey, which it claims is made using traditional Scotch whisky production methods. Another offering is Whiskey Cream Stock, which is a cream liqueur made from Printer's Whiskey and bottled at 17% ABV.

◀ **PRINTER'S 6-YEAR-OLD**
BLEND 40% ABV
A delicate peated whiskey aged in small oak barrels for a faster maturation.

QUEEN ANNE

Scotland
Owner: Chivas Brothers

A good example of an "orphan brand" that has found its way into the portfolio of a larger company and appears to lack any clear role and purpose, Queen Anne was once a leading name from the distinguished Edinburgh blenders Hill, Thomson & Co. It was first produced in 1884 and blended by one William Shaw. Today it belongs to Chivas Brothers. Like so many once-famous and proud brands, Queen Anne has been left bereft and isolated by consolidation in the Scotch whisky industry, steadfastly clinging on in one or more regions where once it was loved and popular.

QUEEN ANNE ▶
BLEND 40% ABV
Not especially characterful, as the flavors are so tightly integrated that it is difficult to discern individual aromas or tastes. A standard blend for mixing.

REBEL YELL

USA

Luxco, St. Louis, Missouri
www.luxco.com

Made at the Bernheim Distillery in Louisville, Rebel Yell is distilled with a percentage of wheat in its mashbill, instead of rye. Whiskey was first made to the Rebel Yell recipe 1849 and, after enjoying popularity in the southern states for many years, the brand was finally released on an international basis during the 1980s. In addition to the standard bottling, there is also a limited-edition Rebel Reserve expression.

◀ **REBEL YELL**
BOURBON 40% ABV
A nose of honey, raisins, and butter leads into a big-bodied bourbon, which again features honey and a buttery quality, along with plums and soft leather. The finish is long and spicier than might be expected from the palate.

REDBREAST

Ireland
Midleton Distillery, Midleton, County Cork
www.irishdistillers.ie

Redbreast was the name that wine merchants Gilbey's gave to the Jameson whiskey that they matured and bottled. The bonded trade was finally phased out in 1968, but Redbreast was so popular that it was allowed to continue well into the 1980s. In the 1990s, Irish Distillers bought the brand from Gilbey's and re-launched the drink as a 12-year-old pure pot still, part-matured in sherry wood. There is also a limited-edition 15-year-old version.

REDBREAST 12-YEAR-OLD ▶
PURE POT STILL 40% ABV
This is, without doubt, one of the world's finest whiskeys. Flavors range from ginger to cinnamon, peppermint to linseed, and licorice to camphor. A sherry note sets off an elegant finish.

REISETBAUER

Austria

Axberg 15, 4062 Kirchberg-Thening
www.reisetbauer.at

Hans Reisetbauer initially made a name for himself as a quality distiller of fruits. Then, in 1995, he decided to start distilling single malt whiskey—growing his own barley, malting, and fermenting on his own premises. The wash is distilled twice in copper pot stills. For maturation, Reisetbauer uses ex-wine casks that previously contained Trockenbeerenauslese and Chardonnay.

◄ REISETBAUER 7-YEAR-OLD
SINGLE MALT 43% ABV
Delicate and multi-layered on the nose, with slightly roasted aromas reminiscent of hazelnuts and dried herbs. Pleasant notes of bread and cereals on the palate. Slightly smoky, with fine spice.

REISETBAUER 12-YEAR-OLD
MALT 48% ABV
Similar to the 7-year-old, with greater emphasis on fruit notes from the wine barrels used for maturation.

RIDGEMONT

USA

Tom Moore Distillery, 1 Barton Road, Bardstown, Kentucky

When this bourbon was introduced to the market in 2004, it was initially called Ridgewood Reserve but, after litigation between the distillers and Woodford Reserve's owners Brown-Forman, the name was changed. The "1792" element of the name pays homage to the year in which Kentucky became a state.

1792 RIDGEMONT RESERVE ►

BOURBON 46.85% ABV

This comparatively delicate and complex 8-year-old small-batch bourbon boasts a soft nose with vanilla, caramel, leather, rye, corn, and spice notes. Oily and initially sweet on the palate, caramel and spicy rye develop along with a suggestion of oak. The finish is oaky, spicy, and quite long, with a hint of lingering caramel.

RITTENHOUSE RYE

USA

Heaven Hill Distillery,
1701 West Breckinridge Street,
Louisville, Kentucky
www.heaven-hill.com

Once associated with Pennsylvania, the rye-whiskey making heartland, Rittenhouse Rye now survives in Kentucky, and its mashbill comprises 51 percent rye, 37 percent corn, and 12 percent barley.

◀ RITTENHOUSE RYE 21-YEAR-OLD

RYE WHISKEY 50% ABV

The nose is notably spicy, with nuts and oranges, while on the palate powerful spices and oak meet lemon and much sweeter notes of lavender and violet. The finish is a long, bitter, rye classic.

RITTENHOUSE RYE 100 PROOF

RYE WHISKEY 50% ABV

Marshmallow and lemon merge on the notably sweet nose, while the lemon carries over into the mouth, where it is joined by black pepper, licorice, and caramel. The finish features dark chocolate and molasses toffee.

ROBERT BURNS

Scotland
Owner: Isle of Arran Distillers
www.arranwhisky.com

With the Scotch whisky industry generally apt to employ Scottish imagery and heritage associations at the drop of a tam-o'-shanter, it is a surprise to find that no one had previously marketed a brand named after Scotland's national bard. Independent distiller Isle of Arran has worked with the World Burns Federation to fill this gap, and now produces an officially endorsed Burns Collection of blended whiskies and malts.

ROBERT BURNS BLEND ▶
BLEND 40% ABV
Hints of oak on the nose give way to sherry, almonds, toffee, and ripe fruits. Plenty of toffee, cake, and dried fruits on the palate, with a light to medium, spicy finish.

ROBERT BURNS SINGLE MALT
SINGLE MALT 40% ABV
A nose of green apples, the acidity tempered by a note of vanilla. Apple and citrus notes on the palate, balanced by vanilla again. An aperitif whisky that is light in style and finish.

ROGUE SPIRITS

USA

Rogue Brewery, 1339 NW Flanders, Portland, Oregon
www.rogue.com

Dead Guy Ale was created in the early 1990s to celebrate the Mayan Day of the Dead (November 1, or All Souls' Day) and, in 2008, the Oregon-based producers launched their Dead Guy Whiskey. It is distilled using the same four malts used in the creation of Dead Guy Ale, and fermented wort from the brewery is taken to the nearby Rogue House of Spirits, where it is double-distilled in a 150-US-gallon (570-liter) copper pot still. A brief maturation period follows, using charred American white-oak casks.

◀ DEAD GUY

BLENDED MALT 40% ABV

Youthful on the nose, with notes of corn, wheat, and fresh, juicy orange. The palate is medium-dry, fruity, and lively. Pepper and cinnamon feature in the finish.

ROSEBANK

Scotland
Camelon, Falkirk

Few Scottish distilleries have managed to stay in continuous production. Many closed during the 1980s and '90s when the industry was dealing with oversupply. Whether a distillery survived when demand picked up depended largely on location. Rosebank, near Falkirk, was closed in 1993 and has since been redeveloped. Founded in 1840, it was chosen to be part of The Ascot Malt Cellar in 1982. Unfortunately for Rosebank, when this became the "Classic Malts" series, Glenkinchie was picked to represent the Lowlands rather than Rosebank.

ROSEBANK DOUGLAS LAING 16-YEAR-OLD ▶

SINGLE MALT: LOWLANDS
50% ABV

This independent bottling from Douglas Laing is part of its Old Malt Cask collection. Despite its strength and age, it is fresh and citrusy.

ROYAL BRACKLA

Scotland
Cawdor, Nairn, Nairnshire

Brackla was founded between the River Findhorn and the Murray Firth by Captain William Fraser in 1812. He was soon complaining that, although he was surrounded by whisky-drinkers, he could only sell 100 gallons (450 liters) a year. By way of compensation, he secured the first royal warrant for a distillery in 1835. Whether he would recognize Royal Brackla today seems unlikely: it was fully modernized in the 1970s and 1990s and now belongs to Bacardi, who launched a 10-year-old in 2004.

◀ ROYAL BRACKLA 10-YEAR-OLD
SINGLE MALT: HIGHLANDS
40% ABV
Aside from a limited-edition 25-year-old, this is the only official bottling. It has a grassy, floral nose and some spicy, oily notes on the tongue.

ROYAL CHALLENGE

India
Owner: United Spirits
www.unitedspirits.in

This "blend of rare Scotch and matured Indian malt whiskeys" is owned by Shaw Wallace, a part of United Spirits since 2005. It is described as "the iconic" premium Indian whiskey and, until 2008, it was also the bestselling premium Indian whiskey, but is now severely challenged by Blenders Pride *(see p56)*.

ROYAL CHALLENGE ▶
BLEND 42.8% ABV
A soft, rounded nose, with traces of malt, nuts, caramel, and a light rubber note. These aromas translate well in the taste at full strength. With water, it remains dense and full-bodied but the taste, diluted, is not as heavy. Very sweet, slightly nutty, and mouth-drying, but with a longish finish.

ROYAL LOCHNAGAR

Scotland

Ballater, Aberdeenshire
www.malts.com

This charming distillery sits alone on Deeside as the only whisky-making business in the area. It was founded in 1845 by John Begg, who wasted no time in asking his new neighbors at Balmoral Castle—Queen Victoria and Prince Albert—to look around his distillery. By the end of 1848, Lochnagar had become Royal Lochnagar. Today it is owned by Diageo.

◀ ROYAL LOCHNAGAR 12-YEAR-OLD

SINGLE MALT: HIGHLANDS
40% ABV

A subtle, leathery nose with a flavor that becomes drier and more acidic before a spicy, sandalwood finish.

ROYAL LOCHNAGAR SELECTED RESERVE

SINGLE MALT: HIGHLANDS
43% ABV

Deep, complex malt with a resinous, sweet, woody character and hints of apple pie and burned sugar.

ROYAL SALUTE

Scotland

Owner: Chivas Brothers

Originally produced by Seagram in 1953 to commemorate the coronation of Queen Elizabeth II, Royal Salute claims to be the first super-premium whisky.

Historically, Chivas Brothers were noted for their exceptional stocks of rare, aged whiskies, and these formed the basis for the Royal Salute expressions. Now controlled by Pernod Ricard, the blenders, led by the highly respected Colin Scott, have access to single malts from well-known distilleries like Glenlivet, Aberlour, Strathisla, and Longmorn.

ROYAL SALUTE 21-YEAR-OLD ▶

BLEND 40% ABV

Soft, fruity aromas balanced with a delicate floral fragrance and mellow, honeyed sweetness.

ROYAL SALUTE, THE HUNDRED CASK SELECTION

BLEND 40% ABV

Elegant, creamy, and exceptionally smooth, with a mellow, oaky, slightly smoky finish.

RUSSELL'S RESERVE

USA

Wild Turkey Distillery, US Highway 62 East, Lawrenceburg, Kentucky
www.wildturkeybourbon.com

Master Distiller Jimmy Russell and his son Eddie, of Wild Turkey fame, developed this small-batch rye whiskey, launched in 2007.

According to Eddie Russell, "we knew the whiskey we wanted, but had never tasted it before. This one really makes the grade—deep character and taste and, at six years, aged to perfection."

◀ RUSSELL'S RESERVE RYE
RYE WHISKEY 45% ABV
Fruity, with fresh oak and almonds on the nose. Full-bodied and robust, yet smooth. Almonds, pepper, and rye dominate the palate, while the finish is long, dry, and characteristically bitter.

RUSSELL'S RESERVE 10-YEAR-OLD
BOURBON 45% ABV
This bourbon boasts a nose of pine, vanilla, soft leather, and caramel. More vanilla, toffee, almond, honey, and coconut in the mouth, and a slightly unusual note of chiles that continues through the lengthy, spicy finish.

SAM HOUSTON

USA

McLain & Kyne Ltd. (Castle Brands), Louisville, Kentucky
www.mclainandkyne.com

McLain & Kyne Ltd. is best known for what it terms "very small batch bourbons," and the firm blends whiskey from as few as eight to twelve barrels of varying ages for their Jefferson's *(see p201)* and Sam Houston bourbon brands.

Sam Houston was introduced in 1999 and is named after the colorful 19th-century soldier, statesman, and politician Samuel Houston, who became the first president of the Republic of Texas.

SAM HOUSTON SMALL BATCH 10-YEAR-OLD ▶

BOURBON (VARIABLE ABV)

The nose offers delicate aromas of red berries, oak, and rye bread, while the rich, tangy palate boasts resin, nutmeg, rye bread, leather, and gentle spice. Long, sweet, and textured in the finish.

SAZERAC RYE

USA

Buffalo Trace Distillery,
1001 Wilkinson Boulevard,
Frankfort, Kentucky
www.buffalotrace.com

Sazerac Rye is part of the annually updated Buffalo Trace Antique Collection and, having been aged for 18 years, is the oldest rye whiskey currently available. According to Buffalo Trace, the 18-year-old 2008 release is comprised of whiskey that has been aging in its warehouse on the first floor, which enables the barrels to age slowly and gracefully.

◄ **SAZERAC RYE 18-YEAR-OLD**
RYE WHISKEY 45% ABV
Rich on the nose, with maple syrup and a hint of menthol. This expression is oily on the palate, fresh, and lively, with fruit, pepper, and pleasing oak notes. The finish boasts lingering pepper, with returning fruit and a final flavor of molasses.

SCAPA

Scotland
St. Ola, Orkney
www.scapamalt.com

Founded in 1885 on "Mainland," the largest of the Orkney islands, Scapa kept going more or less continuously until 1994, when it was shut down. Although production resumed three years later, it was only on a seasonal basis, using staff from its neighbor, Highland Park. For years it seemed there was only room for one viable distillery on Orkney—that being Highland Park—but Scapa's rescue came in the form of Allied Domecq, and over £2m was lavished on it in 2004. The company has since been bought by Chivas Brothers.

SCAPA 14-YEAR-OLD ▶
SINGLE MALT: ISLANDS
40% ABV
Compared to the robust, smoky Highland Park, Scapa is softer and a little sweeter. It has a heathery, dried-fruit character with a gentle spiciness.

SCOTTISH LEADER

Scotland

Owner: Burn Stewart Distillers

The owner describes Scottish Leader as an "international award-winning blend with a honey rich smooth taste profile. It has a growing presence in a number of world markets." The blend's heart is Deanston single malt, from the Perthshire distillery of the same name. Initially targeted at the value-conscious supermarket buyer, Scottish Leader has recently been repackaged and shows signs of an attempted move somewhat upmarket. The blends are now available in non-aged and 12-year-old expressions.

◀ **SCOTTISH LEADER**

BLEND 40% ABV

A standard blend in which the flavor characteristics are tightly integrated. Not much to mark it out, but okay for mixing or drinking on the rocks.

SEAGRAM'S

Canada

Diageo Canada, West Mall, Etobicoke, Ontario
www.diageo.com

Joseph Emm Seagram ran a flour mill in Ontario in the 1860s, where he became interested in distilling as a way of using surplus grains. By 1883 distilling was the core business and Seagram was the sole owner. The brand 83 commemorates this. The VO brand stands for "Very Own" and was once the best-selling Canadian whiskey in the world. Diageo now controls the Canadian Seagram's labels, as well as Seagram's 7 Crown *(see p314)*, which is marketed as an American whiskey.

SEAGRAM'S VO ▶
BLEND 40% ABV
The nose presents pear drops, caramel, and some rye spice, along with butter. Light-bodied, sweet, and lightly spicy, with a slightly acerbic mouthfeel.

SEAGRAM'S 83
BLEND 40% ABV
At one time, this was even more popular than VO. Now it is a standard Canadian: smooth and easy to drink.

SEAGRAM'S 7 CROWN

USA

Angostura Distillery, Lawrenceburg, Indiana

One of the best known and most characterful blended American whiskeys, Seagram's 7 Crown has survived the break-up of the Seagram distilling empire and is now produced by Caribbean-based Angostura (of Angostura Bitters fame). This relative newcomer to the US distilling arena has acquired the former Seagram distillery at Lawrenceburg, where 7 Crown is made, along with the long-shuttered Charles Medley Distillery in Owensboro, Kentucky. The Lawrenceburg distillery is the largest spirits facility in the USA in terms of production capacity.

◀ **SEAGRAM'S 7 CROWN**

BLEND 40% ABV

This possesses a delicate nose with a hint of spicy rye, and is clean and well structured on the spicy palate.

SHEEP DIP

Scotland
Owner: Spencerfield Spirits
www.spencerfieldspirit.com

Sheep Dip is one of the better blended malts. The brand has been around since the 1970s but, under the ownership of Whyte & Mackay, was largely ignored. In 2005, it was taken on by Alex and Jane Nicol, who aim to rebuild the former glory of so-called "orphan brands." Since then, they've introduced new packaging, appointed a global network of agents and, most important of all, reformulated the whisky under the guidance of master blender Richard Paterson. It seems to be working. The whiskies are aged between 8 and 12 years in quality first-fill wood, producing a great dram.

SHEEP DIP ▶
BLENDED MALT 40% ABV
The nose is delicate and refined. Great finesse on the palate, then a majestic assertion of pure malty flavors.

SIGNATURE

India

Owner: United Spirits
www.unitedspirits.in

The recently introduced Signature Rare Aged Whiskey comes from the McDowell's stable, owned by United Spirits, and has the slogan "Success is Good Fun." It is a blend of Scotch and Indian malt whiskeys and is the fastest-growing brand in the company's portfolio. It has also won a clutch of international awards, including a gold in the Monde Selection 2006.

◄ **SIGNATURE**

BLEND 42.8% ABV

A rich nose, with a distinct medicinal note. Straight, the taste is surprisingly sweet, with smoky and medicinal undertones, becoming less sweet with water. Relatively light in body, with a distinct peaty, smoky edge.

SLYRS

Germany

Bayrischzellerstrasse 13 , 83727
Schliersee, Ortsteil Neuhaus
www.slyrs.de

Slyrs was founded in 1999 and makes a credible whiskey, which is distributed by Lantenhammer, a schnapps distillery located in the same village. Slyrs is bottled after maturing for an unspecified time in new American white-oak barrels. In October 2008, Raritas Diaboli, a special cask-strength edition, was launched.

SLYRS ▶

SINGLE MALT 43% ABV

Some flowery aromas and spicy notes deliver a nice and easy dram. The taste varies according to the vintage.

SOMETHING SPECIAL

Scotland
Owner: Chivas Brothers

It's quite a name to live up to, but "something special" is a justifiable claim for this premium blend, which is the third bestselling whisky in South America, with sales of over half a million cases. The blend dates back to 1912, when it was created by the directors of Hill, Thomson & Co. of Edinburgh. The primary component is drawn from Speyside malts, especially the highly regarded Longmorn, which is at the heart of the blend. A 15-year-old version was launched in 2006. The distinctive bottle is said to have been inspired by an Edinburgh diamond-cutter.

◀ **SOMETHING SPECIAL**
BLEND 40% ABV
A distinctive blend of dry, fruity, and spicy flavors, with a subtle, smoky, sweetness on the palate.

SPEYBURN

Scotland

Rothes, Aberlour, Morayshire
www.inverhouse.com

Whether she knew it or not, Queen Victoria's loyal subjects at the newly built Speyburn Distillery near Rothes labored through the night to produce a whisky for her Diamond Jubilee in 1897. It was mid-December and, though the windows were not yet in place and snow was swirling in from outside, the distillery manager ordered the stills to be fired up. Speyburn has retained its Victorian charm and, since 1991, has been owned by Inver House.

SPEYBURN 10-YEAR-OLD ▶

SINGLE MALT: SPEYSIDE
40% ABV

Despite the release of older expressions, including a 25-year-old Solera, the core expression of Speyburn remains the 10-year-old, which has a flavor of vanilla fudge and a sweet, lingering finish.

SPEYSIDE

Scotland
Glen Tromie, Kingussie,
Inverness-shire
www.speysidedistillery.co.uk

With a production of just 130,000 gallons (600,000 liters), the distillery named after Scotland's biggest malt whisky region is no giant. Nor is it all that old. Despite its rustic appearance—only a discreet modern smoke stack belies its youth—Speyside was commissioned in 1962 by the blender and bottler George Christie. Built stone-by-stone, it was not finished until 1987. Among its single malts have been Drumguish (no age-statement) and Speyside 8-, 10-, and 12-year-olds.

◄ SPEYSIDE 12-YEAR-OLD
SINGLE MALT: SPEYSIDE
40% ABV
The flavor of this well-balanced 12-year-old recalls nougat, with a faint smoky edge. It is slightly richer and more full-bodied than you would expect from its restrained nose.

SPRINGBANK

Scotland
Campbeltown, Argyll
www.springbankdistillers.com

Springbank was officially founded in 1823, at a time when there were no fewer than 13 licensed distillers in Campbeltown. Although this end of the Mull of Kintyre stills feels pretty cut off by car, it was always a short hop across the Firth of Clyde to Glasgow by ship. And, as the second city of the British empire boomed, distilleries like Springbank were on hand to quench its ever-growing thirst. In the other direction there was the US but, when that went dry during Prohibition, and the big ☛

SPRINGBANK 15-YEAR-OLD ▶
SINGLE MALT: CAMPBELTOWN
46% ABV
Sweet toffee and candied peel on the nose give way to more exotic sweet-and-sour flavors in the mouth.

SPRINGBANK 10-YEAR-OLD
SINGLE MALT: CAMPBELTOWN
46% ABV
A complex cocktail of flavors, from ripe citrus fruit to peat smoke, vanilla, spice, and a faint underlying salty tang.

SPRINGBANK

blenders turned ever more to Speyside, Campbeltown's demise was swift.

Yet Springbank survived. Much of this must have been down to its continuity: the distillery was originally owned by the Reid family, who sold out to their in-laws, the Mitchells, in the mid-19th century. The Mitchells are still in charge, and have built up a real cult following for their innovative range of single malts.

◀ SPRINGBANK VINTAGE 1997

SINGLE MALT: CAMPBELTOWN
54.9% ABV

A complex nose of toffee mixed with smoky, leathery aromas. Drier on the palate, with a meaty, mouth-filling flavor wreathed in smoke.

SPRINGBANK 100 PROOF

SINGLE MALT: CAMPBELTOWN
57% ABV

A big, full-bodied malt with a dried-fruit and butterscotch flavors, along with traces of spice, nuts, and smoke.

ST. GEORGE

USA

St. George Spirits, 2601 Monarch Street, Alameda, California
www.stgeorgespirits.com

St. George Spirits was established by Jörg Rupf in 1982, and the distillery operates two Holstein copper pot stills. A percentage of heavily roasted barley is used, some of which is smoked over alder and beech wood. Most of the single malt whiskey is put into former bourbon barrels and matured for between three and five years, with a proportion matured in French oak and former port casks.

ST. GEORGE ▶

SINGLE MALT 43% ABV

The nose offers fresh, floral notes, with fruit, nuts, coffee, and vanilla. It is quite delicate on the palate; sweet, nutty, and fruity, with a hint of menthol and cocoa. Vanilla and chocolate notes in the finish, along with gentle smoke.

STEWARTS CREAM OF THE BARLEY

Scotland

Owner: Chivas Brothers

First produced around 1831, this old-established brand is today a topseller in Ireland. For many years it enjoyed great popularity in Scotland, too, not least because of its widespread distribution in public house chain of Allied, the owner at the time. Single malt from Glencadam used to be at the heart of the blend. With changes in ownership, Glencadam is now in other hands, but the blend reputedly still contains a healthy proportion of up to 50 different single malts.

◄ **STEWARTS CREAM OF THE BARLEY**

BLEND 40% ABV

A malty, sweet, soft, and slightly spirity nose. The fruitiness of a young spirit on the palate—raw and a little smoky. Peppery, drying, charred-wood finish.

STRANAHAN'S

USA

Stranahan's Colorado Whiskey,
2405 Blake Street, Denver, Colorado
www.stranahans.com

Jess Graber and George Stranahan established the Denver distillery, the first licensed distillery in Colorado, in March 2004. Whiskey is produced using a four-barley fermented wash produced by the neighboring Flying Dog Brewery. The distillation takes place in a Vendome still, and the spirit is put into new, charred American-oak barrels. It is aged for a minimum of two years, and each bottled batch is composed of the contents of between two and six barrels.

STRANAHAN'S COLORADO WHISKEY ▶

COLORADO WHISKEY 47% ABV

The nose is very bourbon-like, with notes of caramel, licorice, spice, and oak. The palate is slightly oily, big, and sweet, with honey and spices. The fairly short finish is quite oaky.

STRATHISLA

Scotland
Keith, Banffshire
www.maltwhiskydistilleries.com

In 1786, Alexander Milne and George Taylor founded the Milltown Distillery in Keith. The whisky it produced was known as Strathisla and, in 1951, this was adopted as the name for the distillery. Over the years, Strathisla has survived fires, explosions, and bankruptcy, to become the oldest and possibly most handsome distillery in the Highlands, with a high-gabled roof and two pagodas. Bought by Chivas Brothers in 1950, it has been the spiritual home of Chivas Regal ever since.

◀ **STRATHISLA 12-YEAR-OLD**
SINGLE MALT: SPEYSIDE
43% ABV
This has a rich, sumptuous nose and a spicy, fruitcake character, thanks to the influence of sherry. It is medium-bodied, with a slight smoky note on the finish.

STRATHMILL

Scotland
Keith, Banffshire
www.malts.com

With its twin pagoda roof, this handsome late-Victorian distillery was built in 1891 as the Glenisla-Glenlivet Distillery. Four years later it was bought by Gilbey, the London-based gin distiller, and re-christened Strathmill—a reference to the fact that it stood on the site of an old corn mill. A single malt expression was released as early as 1909, but Strathmill's long-term role in life was—and is—to supply malt for blended Scotch, particularly J&B.

STRATHMILL FLORA & FAUNA 12-YEAR-OLD ▶

SINGLE MALT: SPEYSIDE
43% ABV

On the lighter, more delicate side of Speyside, Strathmill has a nutty, malty character with notes of vanilla from the wood. It is quite soft and medium-sweet on the tongue.

SULLIVANS COVE

Australia

Tasmania Distillery, Lamb Place, Cambridge, Tasmania
www.tasmaniadistillery.com.au

Part-owner and Master Distiller Patrick Maguire admits that some of the early batches of spirit were not as good as they should have been, but the whiskey is now winning national awards. Locally grown, unpeated Franklin barley-malt is used. The spirit is brewed at Cascade Brewery, distilled in a Charentais-style pot still, and bottled from single casks by hand.

◀ SULLIVANS COVE PORT MATURATION

SINGLE MALT 60% ABV

This 7-year-old was matured in a French oak ex-port cask. It has a floral nose, developing into rich malty stout; the taste is tannic and warming.

SULLIVANS COVE BOURBON MATURATION

SINGLE MALT 60% ABV

Another 7-year-old, this time from an American oak ex-bourbon cask. It is sweet and malty, with oaky and chocolate notes.

SUNTORY HAKUSHU

Japan
Torihara 2913–1, Hakushucho, Komagun, Yamanashi
www.suntory.co.jp

Located in a forest high in the Japanese Alps, Hakushu was once the largest malt distillery in the world, producing a vast array of different makes for the Suntory blenders; nowhere else offers such an array of shapes and sizes of pot stills. Hakushu single malt seems to echo the location, being light, gentle, and fresh.

SUNTORY HAKUSHU 12-YEAR-OLD ▶

SINGLE MALT 43.5% ABV

A very cool nose, with cut grass, a growing mintiness, and a hint of linseed oil. The palate is sweet but quite slow; the minty, grassy character is given depth by apricot fruitiness and extra fragrance by a camomile note.

SUNTORY HAKUSHU 18-YEAR-OLD

SINGLE MALT 43% ABV

Once again a vegetal note, this time more like a tropical rain forest. There's also plum, mango, hay, and fresh ginger. Good acidity and a toasty, oaky finish.

Whiskey Tour: Japan

Tokyo is a good starting point for the whiskey lover. The city has myriad whiskey bars and excellent train connections to the distilleries at Chichibu, Karuizawa, Hakushu, and Gotemba. Further afield, Suntory's flagship distillery, Yamazaki, is also accessible by train, and can be combined with a visit to Kyoto or Osaka.

DAY 1: CHICHIBU DISTILLERY

❶ **Chichibu**, Japan's newest distillery, started by Ichiro Akuto, has no visitor facilities yet, but whiskey enthusiasts can arrange a personal tour by contacting the distillery in advance *(+81 (0)494 62 4601)*. Chichibu city is 90 minutes by train from Tokyo's Ikebukuro station. A taxi can be taken from the station to the distillery, which is outside the city.

DAYS 2–3: KIRIN'S KARUIZAWA DISTILLERY

❷ The Kirin Distillery in **Karuizawa** is a small whiskey-making plant. It is open to visitors and incorporates an art gallery. Karuizawa is a spa town that is 65–80 minutes by the Nagano Shinkansen from Tokyo Station, or by local train connections from Chichibu (3–5 hours). There are numerous spa resort hotels close to the distillery for those wishing to make an extended break.

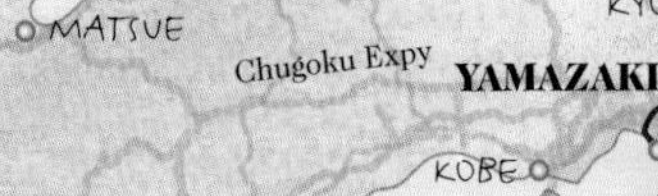

TOUR STATISTICS
DAYS: 8 **LENGTH:** 300 miles (480km) **TRAVEL:** Shinkansen (bullet trains), local trains **DISTILLERIES:** 5

Shinjiro Torii is revered in Japan as the founder of Suntory, which operates the Yamazaki and Hakushu distilleries on this tour.

SENDAI
NIIGATA
FUKUSHIMA
Banetsu Expy
Horukiku Expy
Tohoku Expy
Kanetsu Expy
START
NAGANO
Nagano Shinkansen Line
2 KARUIZAWA
1 CHICHIBU
TOKYO
3 HAKUSHU
JR Chuo Line
JR Asigiri Line
HONSHU
GOTEMBA 4
Tokaido Shinkansen Line
AGOYA
miles
0 30
0 30
kilometres

DAY 4: SUNTORY'S HAKUSHU DISTILLERY

3 **Hakushu** is surrounded by a lovely nature reserve in the southern Japanese Alps. The nearest station is Kobuchizawa, which is accessible by slow trains from Karuizawa, or by express train (JR Chuo Line) from Tokyo's Shinjuku Station.

HAKUSHU DISTILLERY

DAYS 5–6: KIRIN'S GOTEMBA DISTILLERY

4 It is best to access Gotemba by fast train from Tokyo's Shinjuku station. The town is the start of one of the main routes up Mount Fuji, and home to Kirin's **Gotemba** Distillery. Many visitors come to visit both. They start climbing Fuji in the afternoon to reach the 8th or 9th stage by nightfall, where there are huts for pilgrims. The summit is reached at dawn. After descending, it is possible to get a bus back to Gotemba to visit the distillery. Although not the prettiest of distilleries, it has good facilities and a spectacular view of Fuji from its rooftop terrace.

MOUNT FUJI AND TRAIN

DAYS 7–8: SUNTORY'S YAMAZAKI DISTILLERY

5 It is best to take the bullet train to either Kyoto or Osaka to make a base for visiting the Suntory Distillery at **Yamazaki**, the company's original whiskey-making plant. Local trains from either city stop at JR Yamazaki station. There are extensive visitor facilities, including an impressive tasting bar with exclusive bottlings. The distillery offers well-heeled clients a chance to buy a cask through its Owner's Cask scheme. There is also a traditional Shinto shrine to visit.

YAMAZAKI DISTILLERY

SUNTORY HIBIKI

Japan

Torihara 2913–1, Hakushucho, Komagun, Yamanashi
www.suntory.co.jp

The fortunes of Suntory were built on blended whiskies based on malts from its two distilleries: Yamazaki and Hakushu. Although there is a move toward single malts globally, the Hibiki range is still regarded as very important.

◀ SUNTORY HIBIKI 17-YEAR-OLD

BLENDED MALT 43% ABV

This, the original Hibiki, has a soft, generous nose featuring super-ripe fruits, light peatiness, a hint of heavy florals (jasmine), and citrus. On the palate: caramel, black cherry, vanilla, rosehip, and light oak structure.

SUNTORY HIBIKI 30-YEAR-OLD

BLENDED MALT 43% ABV

This multi-award winner is huge in flavor, a compote of different fruits: Seville orange, quince paste, quite assertive wood, and walnuts, followed by aniseed and fennel, and a deep spiciness. The palate is sweet and velvety, with Old English Marmalade to the fore, with sweet, dusty spices.

SUNTORY YAMAZAKI

Japan
Yamazaki 5–2–2, Honcho, Mishimagun, Osaka
www.suntory.co.jp

Established in 1923, Yamazaki was the first malt distillery built in Japan, and was home to the fathers of the nation's whiskey industry, Shinjiro Torii and Masataka Taketsuru. ☛

THE YAMAZAKI 12-YEAR-OLD ▶

SINGLE MALT 43% ABV

The mainstay of the range, the 12-year-old is crisp, with a fresh nose of pineapple, citrus, flowers, dried herbs, and a little oak. The palate is sweet and filled with ripe soft fruits and a hint of smoke.

THE YAMAZAKI 18-YEAR-OLD

SINGLE MALT 43% ABV

With age, Yamazaki acquires more influence from oak. The estery notes of younger variants are replaced by ripe apple, violet, and a deep, sweet oakiness. This impression continues on the palate with a mossy, pinelike character and the classic Yamazaki richness in the middle of the mouth. This is an extremely classy whiskey.

SUNTORY YAMAZAKI

Like Hakushu, it makes a huge range of styles. The official single-malt bottlings focus on the sweet fruity expression. Single-cask bottlings have also been released. Most of the older ones have been aged in ex-sherry casks, but there are some Japanese-oak releases for Japanese malt converts.

◀ SUNTORY VINTAGE 1984

SINGLE MALT 56% ABV

An award-winning, heavily sherried expression. Very dark with a balsamic nose, wood bark, yew, plum pudding, and espresso coffee. The palate has black cherry, molasses toffee, and prune. Interesting mix of bitter and sweet, with strong tannins.

THE CASK OF YAMAZAKI 1990 SHERRY BUTT

SINGLE MALT 61% ABV

One of a regular series of single cask releases, this has an almost opaque mahogany color and a nose filled with date, prune, and figgy sherried notes. Some peatiness adds complexity. The palate is grippy and autumnal with light woodsmoke, walnut, espresso (with sugar), and a long, firm finish that ends with a touch of molasses.

TALISKER

Scotland
Carbost, Isle of Skye
www.taliskerwhisky.com

Talisker, founded in 1830 by Hugh and Kenneth MacAskill, is the only surviving distillery on Skye. Given Skye's size and proximity to the mainland, it seems odd that there is only one distillery there, when Islay has so many.

Talisker struggled through the 19th century until, in 1898, it teamed up with Dailuaine, then the largest distillery in the Highlands. In 1916, the joint venture was taken over by a consortium involving Dewar's, the Distillers Company, ☛

TALISKER 10-YEAR-OLD ▶
SINGLE MALT: ISLANDS
45.8% ABV
An iconic West Coast malt with a pungent, slightly peaty character that has a peppery catch on the finish.

TALISKER 18-YEAR-OLD
SINGLE MALT: ISLANDS
45.8% ABV
Age has softened the youthful vigor of the 10-year-old, and given it a fine scent of leather and aromatic smoke and a creamy, mouth-filling texture.

TALISKER

and John Walker & Sons. Ever since, Talisker has been a key component in Johnnie Walker Red Label.

Until 1928, Talisker was triple-distilled, like an Irish whiskey, which tells why two wash stills are paired to three spirit stills. The lyne arms have a unique U shape to increase reflux and make a cleaner spirit, although the fact that this is then condensed in worm tubs seems contradictory, as worm tubs produce a heavier, more sulfurous spirit. Whatever the rationale, it works, and Talisker has won countless awards and fans.

◀ TALISKER DISTILLERS EDITION 1996

SINGLE MALT: ISLANDS
45.8% ABV

With a maturation that ends in Amoroso sherry casks, the Distillers Edition has a peppery, spicy character, softened by a luscious, dried-fruit richness in the mouth.

TALISKER 57° NORTH

SINGLE MALT: ISLANDS
57% ABV

Named in reference to the latitude of the distillery, this is rich, fruity, smoky, peppery, and spicy, with a long finish.

TAMDHU

Scotland
Knockando, Aberlour, Morayshire
www.edringtongroup.com

While it may keep a low profile, offering just one young distillery bottling, Tamdhu is a large set-up, with nine pine washbacks, three pairs of stills, and a mix of dunnage and racked warehousing on site. There's a maltings plant, too, and part of Tamdhu's role in the Edrington Group is to supply some of the malt for the company's other distilleries, as well as all the malt for its own whisky.

As you might expect of a distillery with only one official expression, there are several independent bottlings of Tamdhu—from Duncan Taylor, Douglas Laing, Gordon & MacPhail, and a 29-year-old from the Douglas Laing Old Malt Cask series.

TAMDHU ▶
SINGLE MALT: SPEYSIDE
40% ABV
Bottled by the distiller to replace the old 8-year-old, this is a youthful introduction to Speyside, with no age statement and a slight peppery edge.

TAMNAVULIN

Scotland
Ballindalloch, Banffshire

In 1966, Invergordon Distillers, now part of Whyte & Mackay, decided to build a big new distillery in a picturesque corner of Upper Speyside by the River Livet. Its six stills could pump out as much as 880,000 gallons (4 million liters) of pure alcohol a year. Yet, in 1995, Tamnavulin closed down—the owners, it seemed, had decided to focus their attention on their other distilleries, Dalmore and Jura in particular. The UB Group bought Whyte & Mackay in 2007, and now Tamnavulin is back up and running.

◄ TAMNAVULIN 12-YEAR-OLD
SINGLE MALT: SPEYSIDE
40% ABV
A light, aperitif-style malt, with a dry, cereal character and minty nose. This standard release of the so-called "Stillman's Dram" is joined by occasional older expressions.

TANGLE RIDGE

Canada

Alberta Distillery, 1521 34th Avenue Southeast, Calgary, Alberta

This whiskey from the Alberta Distillery *(see p12)* is sweeter than its stablemates, although, like the other Alberta whiskeys, it is made exclusively from rye. Introduced in 1996, it is one of the new school of premium Canadian whiskeys: aged 10 years in oak, it is then "dumped" and small amounts of vanilla and sherry are added. The spirit is then re-casked for a time to allow the flavors to marry.

Its name comes from a limestone wall in the Canadian Rockies that was discovered by distinguished explorer, artist, and writer Mary Schaffer (1861–1939).

TANGLE RIDGE DOUBLE CASK ▶

CANADIAN RYE 40% ABV

Butterscotch and burned caramel on the nose, velvet-smooth mouthfeel, and a very sweet taste, with a hint of sherry. Lacks complexity, however.

TÉ BHEAG

Scotland

Owner: The Gaelic Whisky Co.
www.gaelicwhisky.com

Although it is blended and bottled elsewhere in Scotland, this is another brand from the Pràban na Linne company on Skye (The Gaelic Whisky Company). Té Bheag (pronounced *Chey Vek*) means "the little lady" and is the name of the boat in the logo. It is also colloquial Gaelic for a "wee dram." The blend is popular in France and has won medals in international competition. Té Bheag is non chill-filtered, and Islay, Island, Highland, and Speyside malts aged from 8 to 11 years are used in the blend.

◀ **TÉ BHEAG**

BLEND 40% ABV

The nose is fresh, with a citrus note, good richness, a delicate peatiness, and a touch of cereal. Weighty on the palate, with a good touch of licorice, a toffeelike richness, and some peat.

TEACHER'S

Scotland

Owner: Beam Global

This venerable brand can be dated to 1830, when William Teacher opened a grocery shop in Glasgow. Like other whisky entrepreneurs, he soon branched out into the spirits trade. His sons took over, and blending became increasingly important. In 1884 the trademark Teacher's Highland Cream was registered, and this single brand eventually came to dominate the business. The whisky was always forceful in character, built around single malts from Glendronach and Ardmore. Today it continues to prove popular in South America.

TEACHER'S HIGHLAND CREAM ▶

BLEND 40% ABV

Full-flavored, oily, with fudge and caramel notes on the nose, and toffee and licorice on the palate. A well-rounded, smooth texture and a quick finish that leaves the palate refreshed.

TEANINICH

Scotland
Alness, Ross-shire
www.malts.com

Distillery visitors to the Highland village of Alness rarely notice Teaninich as they make their way to its more famous neighbor Dalmore. And yet Teaninich has been quietly distilling away almost constantly since 1817, when it was set up by Captain Hugh Munro.

Teaninich's role was to supply spirit for blending—no one was interested in marketing it as a single malt to whisky-drinkers until 1992, when its owners, UDV, released a 10-year-old expression.

◀ TEANINICH FLORA & FAUNA 10-YEAR-OLD
SINGLE MALT: HIGHLANDS 43% ABV
The only official distillery bottling is polished and grassy, with a predominantly malty flavor.

TEANINICH GORDON & MACPHAIL 1991
SINGLE MALT: HIGHLANDS 46% ABV
A deep amber, fruitcake-flavored malt, with notes of mint, tobacco, cloves, and wood smoke.

TEERENPELI

Finland

Teerenpeli, Hämeenkatu 19, Lahti
www.teerenpeli.com

Teerenpeli Distillery began life in 1998 within a brewery in the city of Lahti, an hour north of Helsinki. In 2002, its owner, Anssi Pyysing, bought a restaurant nearby, and moved the distillery to the former parking ramp beneath it. The distillery used wash from the brewery until 2010, when a new mash tun was installed, as well as a new visitor center. Until now, only 1,760 gallons (8,000 liters) of spirit have been produced each year, but the distillery's capacity is now up to 6,600 gallons (30,000 liters).

TEERENPELI 3-YEAR-OLD NO. 001 ▶
MALT 43% ABV
A lot of grain (barley), vanilla, and oak wood with a slightly thick body.

TEERENPELI 6-YEAR-OLD
MALT 43% ABV
In Finnish, Teerenpeli means "flirtation". True to its name, this malt is soft and seductive, with pound cake and baked apple flavors, an intriguing mix of herbal and spice notes, and a spritzy mouthfeel.

TEMPLETON RYE

USA

East 3rd Street, Templeton, Iowa
www.templetonrye.com

Scott Bush's Templeton Rye whiskey came onto the market in 2006. It is distilled in a 300-US-gallon (1,150-liter) copper pot still before being aged in new, charred-oak barrels.

Bush boasts that his rye is made to a Prohibition-era recipe. During the years of the Great Depression, a group of farmers in the Templeton area started to distill a rye whiskey illicitly in order to boost their faltering agricultural incomes. Soon, "Templeton Rye" achieved a widespread reputation as a high quality spirit.

◄ **TEMPLETON RYE SMALL BATCH**

RYE WHISKEY 40% ABV

Bright, crisp, and mildly sweet on the palate. The finish is smooth, long, and warming.

THOMAS H. HANDY

USA

Buffalo Trace Distillery,
1001 Wilkinson Boulevard,
Frankfort, Kentucky
www.buffalotrace.com

Thomas H. Handy Sazerac is the newest addition to the Buffalo Trace Antique Collection. It is an uncut and unfiltered straight rye whiskey, named after the New Orleans bartender who first used rye whiskey to make the Sazerac Cocktail. According to the distillers, the barrels are aged six years and five months on the fifth floor of Warehouse M—"it's very flavorful and will remind drinkers of fruitcake."

THOMAS H. HANDY SAZERAC 2008 EDITION ▶

RYE WHISKEY 63.8% ABV

Summer fruits and pepper notes on the nose. The palate is a blend of soft vanilla and peppery rye; the finish is long, with oily, spicy oak.

TOBERMORY

Scotland
Tobermory, Isle of Mull
www.tobermory.co.uk

Tobermory's survival has been a small miracle, given that it has spent much of its life lying idle.

It was founded in the 1790s by local businessman John Sinclair, but closed on his death in 1837. It was revived briefly in the 1880s, but operation was sporadic and it closed again between 1930 and 1972. Again, production was sporadic until it was sold to its present owners, Burn Stewart Distillers in 1993.

◀ TOBERMORY 10-YEAR-OLD
SINGLE MALT: ISLANDS
40% ABV

This fresh, unpeated, maritime malt claims to have a slight smoky character, owing to the water from Mull's peat lochans. If true, the effect is subtle.

TOBERMORY 15-YEAR-OLD
SINGLE MALT: ISLANDS
46.3% ABV

The nose has rich fruitcake notes and a trace of marmalade, thanks to aging in sherry casks. The spicy character comes through on the tongue. It is non chill-filtered and cask strength.

TOMATIN

Scotland
Tomatin, Inverness-shire
www.tomatin.com

With 23 stills and a capacity of 2.6 million gallons (12 million liters) of pure alcohol, Tomatin was once the colossus of the malt whisky industry. In 1974, at the time of its expansion, it eclipsed even Glenfiddich, whose capacity remains at 2.2 million gallons (10 million liters).

Tomatin was founded in 1897, and took a while to reach its super-size status. Its two stills were increased to four as recently as 1956; thereafter expansion was rapid until it peaked in the 1970s, just in time for the first big ☛

TOMATIN 12-YEAR-OLD ▶
SINGLE MALT: HIGHLANDS
40% ABV
A mellow, soft-centered Speyside-style malt, which replaced the old core 10-year-old expression back in 2003.

TOMATIN 18-YEAR-OLD
SINGLE MALT: HIGHLANDS
43% ABV
The deep amber hue betrays a strong sherry influence that brings out fruity and cinnamon flavors in the malt.

TOMATIN

post-war slump. Tomatin struggled on as an independent distillery until 1985, when the liquidators arrived. A year later it was sold to two of its long-standing customers—Takara Shuzo and Okara & Co—thus becoming the first Scottish distillery in Japanese hands.

With 11 fewer stills, production has been cut back to 1.1 million gallons (5 million liters), which still allows plenty of capacity for bottling as a single malt. Tomatin's biggest seller is the standard 12-year-old; the 18- and 25-year-olds form part of the core range, while older expressions and specific vintages are released on a more ad hoc basis.

◀ TOMATIN 25-YEAR-OLD
SINGLE MALT: HIGHLANDS
43% ABV
With its simple packaging, this ripe, zesty malt, full of nuts, and spice, is a triumph of substance over style.

TOMATIN 30-YEAR-OLD
SINGLE MALT: HIGHLANDS
49.3% ABV
A voluptuous after-dinner dram with a big, sherried nose and impressive legs.

TOMINTOUL

Scotland
Kirkmichael, Ballindalloch, Grampian
www.tomintouldistillery.co.uk

Tomintoul opened in 1964—a time of great confidence in the industry, with booming sales of blended Scotch. Its role in life was simply to supply malt for these blends. This role continues under Angus Dundee, who bought the distillery in 2000, when it was in need of malt for its own blends *(see p17)*. While single malts account for a small fraction of the 600,000 gallons (3.3 million liters) produced each year, the number of expressions has increased greatly.

TOMINTOUL 10-YEAR-OLD ►
SINGLE MALT: SPEYSIDE
40% ABV

This delicate, aperitif-style malt has some vanilla from the wood and a light cereal character.

TOMINTOUL 16-YEAR-OLD
SINGLE MALT: SPEYSIDE
40% ABV

Extra years give this expression a nuttier, spicier character with orange peel aromas, as well as more depth and a more rounded texture.

TORMORE

Scotland
Advie, Grantown-on-Spey, Morayshire

Built on a grand scale in 1958, Tormore symbolizes the whisky industry's self-confidence at a time when global demand for blended Scotch was growing strongly. With its copper-clad roof and giant chimney stack, the distillery towers up beside the A95 in Speyside. It seems no expense was spared by the architect, Sir Albert Richardson, a past president of the Royal Academy. Tormore is now owned by Chivas Brothers (Pernod Ricard), who released an official 12-year-old bottling in 2004.

◀ TORMORE 12-YEAR-OLD
SINGLE MALT: SPEYSIDE
40% ABV
There is a soft, malty character to the nose, with notes of melon and grass. In the mouth it has a slightly oily texture and a medium-light body that dries on the finish.

TULLAMORE DEW

Ireland
www.tullamoredew.com

In 1901, the worldwide sales of Irish whiskey peaked at 10 million cases, around the period that the Williams family gained control of Tullamore Distillery. D. E. Williams's name is still associated with the whiskey in Tullamore; as in Tullamore DEW-illiams.

But by 1954, the distillery closed and the brand was sold repeatedly. Now, the whiskey is all made to order in Midleton and it sells very well across continental Europe.

TULLAMORE DEW ▶
BLEND 40% ABV
This whiskey is fairly one-dimensional. It has a characteristic bourbon burn, with not much else to recommend it.

TULLAMORE DEW 12-YEAR-OLD
BLEND 40% ABV
A considerable step up from the other Tullamore blends, the 12-year-old is reminiscent of a premium Jameson. The precious trinity of pot still, sherry, and oak is very much in evidence.

TULLIBARDINE

Scotland
Blackford, Perthshire
www.tullibardine.com

Tullibardine was a mothballed distillery until it was bought by an independent consortium. It soon launched its first official bottling—a 10-year-old—but it will be 2014 before the whisky actually distilled by the new owners sees the light of day. In the meantime there has been a raft of releases based on the inventory inherited in 2003, which included some 3,000 casks dating back to 1952.

◀ TULLIBARDINE 1993 SHERRY WOOD FINISH

SINGLE MALT: HIGHLANDS
46% ABV

Eighteen months in Oloroso sherry butts give this malt a deep amber color and a spicy butterscotch flavor that finishes dry.

TULLIBARDINE 1993

SINGLE MALT: HIGHLANDS
40% ABV

This is more akin to a delicate Speyside than a robust Highland malt. Light citrus nose with a vanilla sweetness from maturation in bourbon casks.

TYRCONNELL

Ireland

Cooley Distillery, Riverstown,
Cooley, County Louth
www.cooleywhiskey.com

It would be hard to find anyone who remembers the original Old Tyrconnell whiskey. The distillery that produced it, Andrew A. Watt and Company of Derry City, closed in 1925. In its day, this whiskey (named after a race horse) was very popular in the US, and early film of baseball games at the Yankee Stadium show billboards advertising "Old Tyrconnel."

But the combined effects of civil unrest in Ireland and Prohibition in the US pushed Watt and many other Irish distilleries into ☛

TYRCONNELL SINGLE MALT ►

SINGLE MALT 40% ABV

Cooley's bestselling malt and it's easy to see why. This has the loveliest nose of any Irish whiskey, releasing jasmine, honeysuckle, and malted-milk cookies.

TYRCONNELL PORT CASK

SINGLE MALT 46% ABV

Port changes the nose slightly, spicing things up. The body has aromas of fig pastry and plum pudding.

TYRCONNELL

☛ the hands of the Scottish United Distillers Company. To protect their core Scotch brands, UDC ruthlessly closed every Irish distillery they bought, bringing the industry across the island to its knees. However, The Tyrconnell was the first brand Cooley's John Teeling chose to bring back to life when he bottled his first single malt in 1992. Since then, various wood finishes have been tried on the 10-year-old.

◀ TYRCONNELL SHERRY CASK
SINGLE MALT 46% ABV
The best of the wood finishes—malt and fruity sherry fuse beautifully.

TYRCONNELL MADEIRA CASK
SINGLE MALT 46% ABV
Madeira and Ireland do each other proud here. Warm hints of cinnamon and mixed spice dance on the palate.

UBERACH

France
Bertrand Distillery,
3 rue du Maréchal Leclerc, BP 21,
67350 Uberach, Alsace
www.distillerie-bertrand.com

The Bertrand brandy and liqueur distillery in Alsace dates from 1874 and has been run by the same family ever since. The Alsace region is blessed with particularly fertile, alluvial soil and the area around the distillery produces a range of fruits that are used in some of Bertrand's spirits. The company has recently branched out to produce beer and two non-filtered whiskies, Uberach Single Malt and Uberach Single Cask.

UBERACH SINGLE MALT ▶
SINGLE MALT 42.2% ABV
Floral, fruity, and spicy, with black tea and hints of plums, as well as wax, and tobacco notes. Aromatic, with good balance and an oaky, fruity finish.

USHER'S GREEN STRIPE

Scotland
Owner: Diageo

One of the foremost names in Scotch whisky, the Edinburgh firm of Usher was a pioneer in the art of blending. In fact, it is recognized for introducing the first modern blend—Old Vatted Glenlivet in 1853. After the firm joined the DCL in 1919, the brand slowly faded away. Today Usher's Green Stripe is among the lowest-priced Scotch available to drinkers in the US, few of whom will either know or care about its distinguished history. But, Usher's whisky remains highly desirable among historians and collectors, owing mostly to the very high standard of its promotional give-away materials.

◀ **USHER'S GREEN STRIPE**
BLEND 40% ABV
A low-priced blend with a high grain content; well-suited to mixing.

VAN WINKLE

USA
2843 Brownsboro Road
Louisville, Kentucky
www.oldripvanwinkle.com

The legendary Julian P. "Pappy" Van Winkle Sr. was a salesman for W. L. Weller & Sons who went on to become famous for his Old Fitzgerald bourbon.

Van Winkle specializes in small-batch, aged whiskeys. The bourbons are made with wheat, rather than cheaper rye. This is said to give the whiskeys a smoother, sweeter flavor during the long maturation period ☛

PAPPY VAN WINKLE'S FAMILY RESERVE 15-YEAR-OLD ▶

BOURBON 53.5% ABV

A sweet caramel and vanilla nose, with charcoal and oak. Full-bodied, round, and smooth in the mouth, with a long and complex finish of spicy orange, toffee, vanilla, and oak.

OLD RIP VAN WINKLE 10-YEAR-OLD

BOURBON 45% ABV

Caramel and molasses on the big nose, then honey and rich, spicy fruit on the profound, mellow palate. The finish is long, with coffee and licorice notes.

VAN WINKLE

favored by Van Winkle. All the whiskeys are matured for at least 10 years in lightly charred mountain oak barrels.

Buffalo Trace *(see p66)* has been in partnership with Julian Van Winkle, "Pappy" Van Winkle's grandson, since 2002, making and distributing his whiskeys. The current expressions were produced at several distilleries, and matured at the Van Winkle's now silent Old Hoffman Distillery.

◀ VAN WINKLE FAMILY RESERVE RYE 13-YEAR-OLD

RYE WHISKEY 47.8% ABV

An almost uniquely aged rye. Powerful nose of fruit and spice. Vanilla, spice, pepper, and cocoa in the mouth. A long finish pairs caramel with black coffee.

PAPPY VAN WINKLE'S FAMILY RESERVE 20-YEAR-OLD

BOURBON 45.2% ABV

Old for a bourbon, this has stood the test of time. Sweet vanilla and caramel nose, plus raisins, apples, and oak. Rich and buttery in the mouth, with molasses and a hint of char. The finish is long and complex, with a touch of oak charring.

VAT 69

Scotland

Owner: Diageo

At its peak, VAT 69 was the 10th-bestselling whisky in the world, and references to it crop up in films and books from the 1950s and 60s. It was launched in 1882 and was once the flagship brand of the independent South Queensferry blenders William Sanderson & Co, its name coming from the fact that vat 69 was the finest of 100 possible blends tested. Today its current owner, Diageo, gives precedence to Johnnie Walker and J&B, and it might not be unreasonable to suggest that—despite sales of more than 1 million cases a year in Venezuela, Spain, and Australia—VAT 69's glory days are behind it.

VAT 69 ▶

BLEND 40% ABV

A light and well-balanced standard blend with an initial, noticeably sweet impact of vanilla ice cream, and a pleasantly malty background.

W. L. WELLER

USA

Buffalo Trace Distillery,
1001 Wilkinson Boulevard,
Frankfort, Kentucky
www.buffalotrace.com

Distilled by Buffalo Trace, W. L. Weller is made with wheat as the secondary grain, for an extra smooth taste.

William Larue Weller was a prominent 19th-century Kentucky distiller, whose company ultimately merged with that of the Stitzel brothers in 1935. A new Stitzel-Weller Distillery was subsequently constructed in Louisville.

◀ W. L. WELLER SPECIAL RESERVE

BOURBON 45% ABV

Fresh fruit, honey, vanilla, and toffee characterize the nose, while the palate has lots of flavor, featuring ripe corn and spicy oak. The medium-length finish displays sweet, cereal notes and pleasing oak.

WALDVIERTLER

Austria
Whiskydestillerie J. Haider OG,
3664 Roggenreith 3
www.roggenhof.at

The Waldviertler Distillery makes two single malts—J. H. Single Malt and J. H. Special Single Malt "Karamell"— and three rye whiskeys—J. H. Original Rye, J. H. Pure Rye Malt, and J. H. Special Pure Rye Malt "Nougat."

Waldviertler uses casks made from the local Manharstberger oak trees. The whiskeys are matured for three to twelve years and offered as single-cask bottlings. Other spirits made here are vodka, gin, and brandy, but—unusually for a European distillery—whiskey is the main focus.

WALDVIERTLER J. H. SPECIAL PURE RYE MALT "NOUGAT" ▶
RYE WHISKEY 41% ABV
A gentle, sweet taste of honey, harmonizing perfectly with the light vanilla taste.

WALDVIERTLER J. H. SPECIAL SINGLE MALT "KARAMELL"
SINGLE MALT 41% ABV
Smoky and dry, with an intense caramel flavor.

WAMBRECHIES

France
1 Rue de la Distillerie,
59118 Wambrechies,
Nord-Pas-de-Calais
www.wambrechies.com

Wambrechies was founded in 1817 as a *jenever* (gin) distillery and is one of only three stills left in the region. It continues to produce an impressive range of *jenevers*, as well as one malt whiskey and a *jenever* beer. Wambrechie whiskeys are bottled at three and eight years old, with the younger whiskey consisting of a lighter, floral blend and the older having a deeper, spicy character.

◄ **WAMBRECHIES 8-YEAR-OLD**
SINGLE MALT 40% ABV
Delicate nose, with aniseed, fresh paint, vanilla, and cereal notes. Smooth on the palate, with a fine, malty profile. Spicy finish, with powdered ginger and milk chocolate.

WHISKY CASTLE

Switzerland
Schlossstrasse 17, 5077 Elfingen
www.whisky-castle.com

Käsers Schloss (the Swiss name of the distillery) is owned by Ruedi and Franziska Käser. The couple started producing whiskey in 2000 and expanded the business in 2006 to include themed events such as whiskey dinners and whiskey conferences at their premises. The brand name of their whiskey in English is Whisky Castle, and there are a number of expressions, including Doublewood, which has a whiff of chestnut, and Edition Käser, which is matured in new Bordeaux casks.

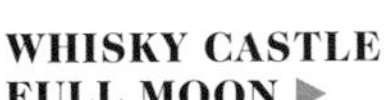

WHISKY CASTLE FULL MOON ▶

SINGLE MALT 43% ABV

Made from smoked barley during the full moon, this is a young whiskey with a sweetish aroma and taste.

WHITE HORSE

Scotland
Owner: Diageo

In its heyday, White Horse was one of the world's top ten whiskies, selling more than 2 million cases a year. Its guiding genius was "Restless" Peter Mackie, described in his day as "one-third genius, one-third megalomaniac, and one-third eccentric." He took over the family firm in 1890 and built an enviable reputation as a gifted blender and entrepreneur.

White Horse is still marketed in more than 100 countries. A deluxe 12-year-old version, White Horse Extra Fine, is occasionally seen.

◄ **WHITE HORSE**
BLEND 40% ABV
Complex and satisfying, White Horse retains the robust flavor of Lagavulin, assisted by renowned Speysiders such as Aultmore. With its long finish, this is a stylish, intriguing blend of crisp grain, clean malt, and earthy peat.

WHYTE & MACKAY

Scotland
www.whyteandmackay.co.uk

The Glasgow-based firm of Whyte & Mackay started blending in the late 19th century. Its flagship Special brand quickly established itself as a Scottish favorite, and remains so to this day. Having been through a bewildering number of owners and a management buy-out in recent years, the company was acquired in May 2007 by the Indian conglomerate UB Group.

One constant through all these changes has been the highly regarded master blender, ☛

WHYTE & MACKAY SPECIAL ▶
BLEND 40% ABV
The nose is full, round, and well-balanced. On the palate, honeyed soft fruits in profusion; smooth and rich, with a long finish.

WHYTE & MACKAY THE THIRTEEN
BLEND 40% ABV
Full, firm, and rich nose, with a slight hint of sherry wood. "Marrying" for a full year before bottling gives great backbone. A well-integrated blend.

WHYTE & MACKAY

Richard Paterson, who joined the firm in 1970 and has received a great number of awards. As well as creating the "new" 40-year-old, Paterson has overseen several aged innovations.

The backbone of the blends emanates from Speyside and the Highlands. Dalmore and—to a lesser extent—Isle of Jura are the company's flagship single malts, and Dalmore's influence can be felt in the premium blends. All the blends are noticeably smooth and well-balanced.

◀ WHYTE & MACKAY 30-YEAR-OLD

BLEND 40% ABV

The flagship of the Whyte & Mackay range is a big, rich, oaky whisky with a deep mahogany hue. The sherry influence is strong, with a pepperiness mellowed by the sweeter flavors.

WHYTE & MACKAY OLD LUXURY

BLEND 40% ABV

A rich bouquet, with malty notes and a subtle sherry influence. It all blends smoothly on the palate. Mellow and silky textured. Warming finish.

THE WILD GEESE

Ireland

www.thewildgeese-irishwhiskey.com

The term "Wild Geese" refers to those Irish nobles and soldiers who left to serve in continental European armies from the late 17th century to the dawn of the 20th century.

The name has come down through history to embrace all the men and women who left Ireland in the last 400 years—not just the nobles. The idea of diaspora and emigration has, of course, been a poignant theme in Irish culture and remains so today. Wild Geese raises a glass to this part of Irish history, and they've produced a good whiskey for the job.

THE WILD GEESE CLASSIC BLEND ▶

BLEND 40% ABV

A hard candy nose. The malt doesn't have much impact here, leaving the grain to carry things to the finish.

THE WILD GEESE RARE IRISH

BLEND 43% ABV

A rich and malty blend, with some spiciness and lemon notes in the body. You'll find a little dry oak in the finish.

WILD TURKEY

USA

Wild Turkey Distillery, US Highway 62 East, Lawrenceburg, Kentucky
www.wildturkeybourbon.com

The Boulevard Distillery is situated on Wild Turkey Hill, above the Kentucky River, near Lawrenceburg. The distillery was first established in 1905 by the three Ripy brothers, whose family had been making whiskey since the year 1869.

◄ WILD TURKEY 80 PROOF

BOURBON 40% ABV

The soft, sweet nose hints at corn, while on the palate this is a very traditional whiskey, nicely balancing caramel and vanilla flavors. Ideal served on the rocks or with a mixer.

WILD TURKEY 101 PROOF

BOURBON 50.5% ABV

Jimmy Russell maintains that 50.5% ABV (101 proof) is the optimum bottling strength for Wild Turkey. This has a remarkably soft yet rich aroma for such a high-proof whiskey. Full-bodied, rich, and robust palate, with vanilla, fresh fruit, spice, brown sugar, and honey. Notes of oak develop in the long and powerful, yet smooth, finish.

The Wild Turkey brand was conceived in 1940, when Austin Nichols' president, Thomas McCarthy, chose a quantity of 101 proof straight bourbon from his company stocks to take along on a wild turkey shoot. Today, Wild Turkey is distilled under the watchful eyes of legendary Master Distiller Jimmy Russell and his son Eddie. The Russells have also created some other highly regarded brands, including Russell's Reserve and American Spirit.

WILD TURKEY RARE BREED ▶
BOURBON (VARIABLE ABV)
A complex, initially assertive nose, with nuts, oranges, spices, and floral notes. Honey, oranges, vanilla, tobacco, mint, and molasses make for an equally complex palate. A long, nutty finish, with spicy, peppery rye.

WILD TURKEY KENTUCKY SPIRIT
BOURBON 50.5% ABV
A single barrel whiskey with a fresh, attractive nose of oranges and notes of rye. Complex on the palate, with almonds, honey, toffee, more oranges, and a hint of leather. The finish is long and sweet, gradually darkening and becoming more syrupy.

Whiskey Tour: Kentucky

The state of Kentucky is the bourbon-producing heartland of the US and home to many of the best-known names in American whiskey. Most of the distilleries offer visitor facilities, allowing guests to study this historic spirit. Touring them is a great way to experience the beauty of Kentucky.

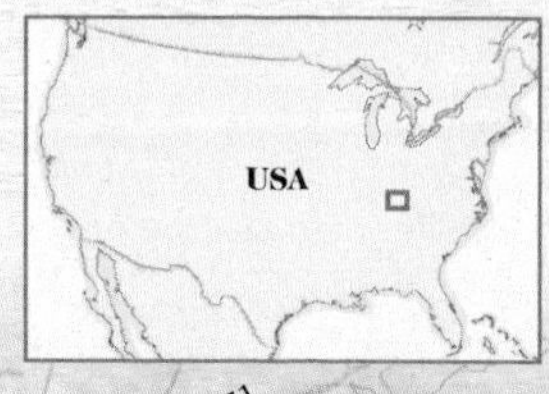

DAY 1: BUFFALO TRACE, WOODFORD RESERVE

BARRELS AT WOODFORD RESERVE

❶ Frankfort, the state capital, has a range of hotels and restaurants, and is the home of **Buffalo Trace**. The distillery's large visitor center offers tours throughout the year.

❷ **Woodford Reserve** lies near the attractive town of Versailles, in Kentucky's famous "blue grass" horse-breeding country. Its copper pot stills are the highlight of the distillery tour.

DAY 2: WILD TURKEY, FOUR ROSES

❸ Spectacularly situated on a hill above the Kentucky River, **Wild Turkey's** Boulevard Distillery allows visitors into its production areas at most times of the year.

❹ **Four Roses** Distillery is a striking structure, built in the style of a Spanish Mission. Tours are available from fall to spring (the distillery is closed throughout the summer). You can also pre-arrange to visit Four Roses' warehouse at Cox's Creek.

WILD TURKEY EMBLEM

TOUR STATISTICS

DAYS: 5
LENGTH: 85 miles (137km)
TRAVEL: Car
DISTILLERIES: 8

DAY 3: HEAVEN HILL, BARTON, OSCAR GETZ

5 Bardstown is renowned as the "World Capital of Bourbon," and makes an excellent base for visiting the distilleries in the area. Book a room at the Old Talbott Tavern, which offers a well-stocked bourbon bar. Then head out to the **Heaven Hill** Bourbon Heritage Center, which includes a tour of a bourbon-aging rackhouse and the chance to taste two Heaven Hill whiskeys.

HEAVEN HILL, BARDSTOWN

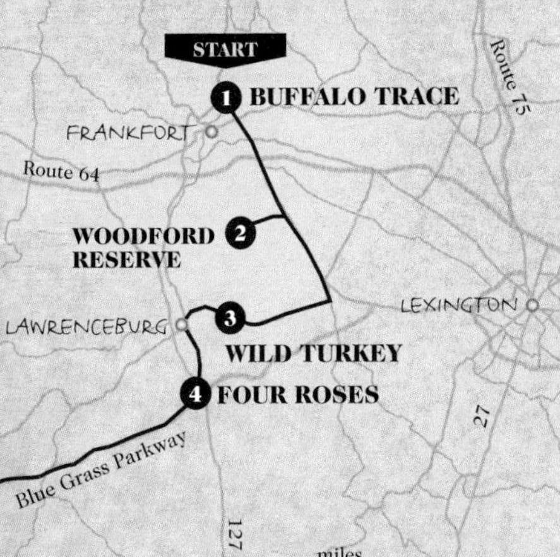

6 The Tom Moore Distillery in Bardstown, which produces the former **Barton** brands, has traditionally maintained a low profile compared to its neighbors. Nowadays, it boasts a state-of-the-art visitor center and in-depth tours of the production areas.

7 A few blocks from Tom Moore, the **Oscar Getz** Whiskey Museum houses a collection of whiskey artefacts, including rare antique bottles, a moonshine still, and Abraham Lincoln's original liquor license.

DAY 4: MAKER'S MARK

8 The historic **Maker's Mark** Distillery stands on the banks of Hardin's Creek, near Loretto, in Marion County. The distillery grounds are notable, being home to some 275 species of trees and shrubs. Guided distillery tours are available daily.

DAY 5: JIM BEAM

9 **Jim Beam**'s Clermont Distillery offers tours of the site grounds, a working rackhouse, and the Hartmann Cooperage Museum. The American Outpost is an on-site visitor center, with a film about the bourbon-making process at Jim Beam and displays of whiskey memorabilia that take in more than two centuries of bourbon history.

JIM BEAM'S CLERMONT DISTILLERY

WILLIAM LAWSON'S

Scotland

Owner: John Dewar & Sons (Bacardi)

Although the Lawson's brand dates back to 1849, the "home" distillery today is MacDuff, built in 1960. Lawson's is managed alongside its big brother, Dewar's, and sells well over 1 million cases a year in France, Belgium, Spain, and parts of South America.

Glen Deveron single malt from MacDuff features heavily in the blend. MacDuff uses the highest percentage of sherry wood of any whisky in the Dewar's group, making the Lawson house style full in flavor and rich golden in color.

◄ WILLIAM LAWSON'S FINEST

BLEND 40% ABV

Slightly dry nose, with delicate oak notes. Well-balanced palate, with hints of crisp candy apple. With a medium to full body, this punches above its weight.

WILLIAM LAWSON'S SCOTTISH GOLD 12-YEAR-OLD

BLEND 40% ABV

Fuller-flavored than the standard Lawson's expression, suggesting a higher malt content.

WINDSOR

Scotland
Owner: Diageo

The name Windsor is an overt link to the British royal family, and the brand's packaging underlines its luxury position, especially in the highly competitive South Korean market. Windsor was originally developed in a partnership between Seagram and local Korean producer Doosan; later Diageo acquired the Seagram interest and launched Windsor 17 as the first super-premium whisky in 2000. Windsor 17's sweeping popularity in Korea posed a threat to its competitors, many of whom have since emulated the older style.

WINDSOR 12-YEAR-OLD ▶
BLEND 40% ABV
Vanilla, wood, and light fresh fruit on the nose. Green apples on the palate, with honey, more vanilla, and spiciness that mellows into a smooth finish.

WINDSOR 17-YEAR-OLD
BLEND 40% ABV
A rich vanilla crème brûlée nose, with fruit and a background layer of malt. Fresh fruit and honey on the palate, with creamy vanilla oak notes.

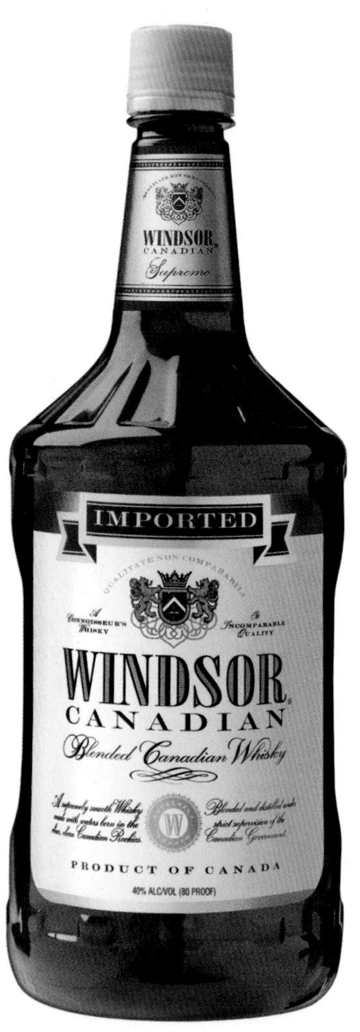

WINDSOR CANADIAN

Canada

Alberta Distillery, 1521 34th Avenue Southeast, Calgary, Alberta

One might think that this comes from the Hiram Walker Distillery in Windsor, Ontario; actually, it is made at the Alberta Distillery *(see p12)*. The name is no doubt meant to recall the British Royal Family, but it should not be confused with the Scotch Windsor *(see p373)*. Like other whiskeys made in Alberta, Windsor Canadian is exclusively rye-based.

◀ WINDSOR CANADIAN

BLENDED CANADIAN RYE 40% ABV

Honey, peaches, pine nuts, and cloves on the nose. A medium body and a sweet taste, with cereal and wood notes. An unassuming whiskey; great value for money.

WISER'S

Canada

Hiram Walker Distillery, Riverside Drive East, Walkerville, Ontario
www.wisers.ca

John Philip Wiser may well have been the first distiller to use the term "Canadian Whiskey" on his label, at the Chicago World's Fair in 1893. By the early 1900s, his was the third largest distillery in Canada, and its whiskeys were being exported to Asia and the US.

A few years after the death of J. P. Wiser in 1917, the company was acquired by Hiram Walker. Eventually, production moved to the Hiram Walker Distillery at Walkerville. Today Wiser's are the fifth best-selling Canadian whiskeys in Canada.

WISER'S DELUXE ▶
BLEND 40% ABV
A fruity and spicy nose, with cereal and linseed oil, vanilla, and toffee.

WISER'S SMALL BATCH
BLEND 43.4% ABV
This is full-flavored, with vanilla, oak, and butterscotch on the nose and in the taste. The slightly higher strength makes for more flavor and texture.

WOODFORD RESERVE

USA

7855 McCracken Pike,
Versailles, Kentucky
www.woodfordreserve.com

Woodford Reserve is the smallest distillery operating in Kentucky, and it is unique among bourbon distilleries because it uses a triple distillation method and three copper pot stills.

◀ WOODFORD RESERVE DISTILLER'S SELECT

BOURBON 45.2% ABV

An elegant yet robust nose, perfumed, with milk chocolate raisins, dried fruit, burned sugar, ginger, and saddle soap. Equally complex on the palate: fragrant and fruity, with raspberries, camomile, and ginger. Lingering vanilla and peppery oak in the finish.

MASTER'S COLLECTION FOUR GRAIN

BOURBON 46.2% ABV

Spicy apple pie, vanilla, caramel, and mint on the nose. The palate features more vanilla, caramel, orange, nuts, and oak. The lengthy finish exhibits pine and spicy oak. The four grains used are corn, malted barley, rye, and wheat.

In 2005, the first bottling in the Master's Collection range was released under the Four Grain Bourbon name, and two years later, a Sonoma-Cutrer Finish was added to the line-up. The Master's Collection 1838 Sweet Mash was released in 2008 to commemorate the year the present Woodford Reserve Distillery was constructed, and to also celebrate the historic "sweet mash" method of bourbon production.

MASTER'S COLLECTION SONOMA-CUTRER FINISH ▶

BOURBON 43.2% ABV

The first and only bourbon in the world to be finished in California Chardonnay barrels. The influence of the wine casks is very apparent in this fruity, sweet bourbon. Butterscotch and almonds on the nose; baked apples, peaches, and toffee in the mouth. Medium to long finish.

MASTER'S COLLECTION 1838 SWEET MASH

BOURBON 43.2% ABV

Maple syrup, spicy fruit, cinnamon, and nutmeg aromas. Rich palate, with more maple syrup, rich fruit, rye, and mint. Lengthy finish, with soft apple notes.

A–Z OF WHISKEYS BY TYPE

Page numbers in *italics* indicate whiskey tour references.

A–Z OF WHISKEYS BY COUNTRY

Page numbers in *italics* indicate whiskey tour references.

ACKNOWLEDGMENTS

Editor-in-Chief Charles MacLean has been researching, writing, and lecturing on whiskey for 30 years. Hailed by *The Times* as "Scotland's leading whisky expert", he is the author of over 10 books on the subject, including *Scotch Whisky: A Liquid History*, *Scotch Whisky*, *Malt Whisky*, and he was Editor-in-Chief of DK's *World Whiskey* (2009). He was also Founding Editor of *Whisky Magazine*. In 2009, Charles was elected Master of the Quaich, the Scotch whisky industry's supreme honour.

Contributors: Dave Broom (Japan) • Tom Bruce-Gardyne (Scotland's malts) Ian Buxton (Scotland's blends) • Charles MacLean (Canada, Australasia, Asia) Peter Mulryan (Ireland) • Hans Offringa (Europe) • Gavin D. Smith (USA).

The publishers would like to thank the following people and organizations for their help in the preparation of this book: Susan Bosanko for indexing, Robert Sharman for editing, Ann Miller at Aberlour Distillery, Rob, Robbie, and Brian at Balvenie and Glenfiddich distilleries, Dave and Heather at Bowmore Distillery, Mark and Duncan at Bruichladdich Distillery, Ewan Mackintosh at Caol Ila Distillery, Ian and Claire at Gordon & MacPhail, Ruth and Ian (Pinky) at Lagavulin Distillery, staff at The Mash Tun in Aberlour, Philip Shorten at Milroy's of Soho, The Whisky Shop Dufftown, Sukhinder Singh and staff at The Whisky Exchange, London (www.thewhiskyexchange.com), Marisa Renzullo, Casper Morris, Becky Offringa of The Whisky Couple.

Image credits: The publishers would like to thank the following producers for their assistance with this project and kind permission to reproduce their photographs in this book and related works:

Aberfeldy Distillery; Aberlour Distillery; Alberta Distillery: Alberta, Tangle Ridge, Windsor Canadian; Allied Distillers; Anchor Distilling Company: Old Potrero; Angus Dundee; Ardbeg Distillery; Ardmore Distillery; Arran Distillers: Arran, Lochranza; Auchroisk Distillery; Aultmore Distillery; Bacardi & Company: Dewar's, Royal Brackla, William Lawson's; Bakery Hill Distillery; Balblair Distillery; The Balvenie Distillery Company; Beam Global España: DYC; Beam Global Distribution (UK): Ardmore, Laphroaig, Teacher's; Beam Global Spirits & Wine, Inc. (USA): Baker's® Kentucky Straight Bourbon Whiskey (53.5% Alc./Vol. ©CST), James B. Beam Distilling Co., Clermont, KY; Basil Hayden's® Kentucky Straight Bourbon Whiskey (40% Alc./Vol. ©CST), Kentucky Springs Distilling Co., Clermont, KY; Booker's® Kentucky Straight Bourbon Whiskey (60.5% - 63.5% Alc./Vol. ©CST), James B. Beam Distilling Co., Clermont, KY; Clermont Distillery; Canadian Club® Blended Canadian Whisky (40% alc./vol. ©CST) Canadian Club Import Company, Deerfield, IL; Jim Beam Black® Kentucky Straight Bourbon Whiskey (43% Alc. Vol. ©CST), James B. Beam Distilling Co., Clermont, KY; Jim Beam® Kentucky Straight Bourbon Whiskey (40% Alc Vol. ©2009), James B. Beam Distilling Co., Clermont, KY; Jim Beam's Choice® Kentucky Straight Bourbon Whiskey (40% Alc./Vol. ©2009), James B. Beam Distilling Co., Clermont, KY; Jim Beam® Straight Rye Whiskey (40% Alc./Vol. ©CST), James B. Beam Distilling Co., Clermont, KY; Kessler® American Blended Whiskey Lightweight Traveler® (40% Alc./Vol. 72.5% Grain Neutral Spirits, ©2009), Julius Kessler Company, Deerfield, IL; Knob Creek® Kentucky Straight Bourbon Whiskey (50% Alc./Vol. ©2009), Knob Creek Distillery, Clermont, KY; Maker's Mark® Bourbon

Whisky (45% Alc./Vol. ©CST), Maker's Mark Distillery, Inc., Loretto, KY; Old Crow® Kentucky Straight Bourbon Whiskey (40% Alc./Vol. ©2009), W.A. Gaines, Div. of The Old Crow Distillery Company, Frankfort, KY; Old Grand-Dad® Kentucky Straight Bourbon Whiskey (43%, 50% and 57% Alc./Vol. ©2009), The Old Grand-Dad Distillery Company, Frankfort, KY; Old Taylor® Kentucky Straight Bourbon Whiskey (40% Alc./Vol. ©CST), The Old Taylor Distillery Company, Frankfort, KY; Benriach Distillery; Benrinnes Distillery; Benromach Distillery; Berry Brothers & Rudd: Cutty Sark; Bertrand Distillery: Uberach; Betta Milk Cooperative: Hellyers Road; Bowmore Distillery; Braunstein; Brown-Forman Corporation: Canadian Mist, Early Times, Old Forester, Woodford Reserve, Jack Daniel's; Bruichladdich Distillery; Bunnahabhain Distillery; Burn Stewart Distillers: Black Bottle, Deanston, Scottish Leader; The Old Bushmills Distillery Co: Bushmills, The Irishman, Knappogue Castle; Campari Drinks Group: Glen Grant, Old Smuggler; Cardhu Distillery; Castle Brands Inc.: Jefferson's, Sam Houston; Chivas Brothers: 100 Pipers, Ballantine's, Chivas Regal, Clan Campbell, Long John, Passport, Queen Anne, Royal Salute, Something Special, Stewarts Cream of the Barley, Strathisla, Tormore; Clear Creek Distillery: McCarthy's; Clontarf Distillery; Clynelish Distillery; Compass Box Delicious Whisky; Constellation Spirits Inc.: Black Velvet®; Cooley Distillery: Connemara, Cooley, Greenore, Inishowen, Kilbeggan, Locke's, Magilligan, Tyrconnel, Wild Geese; Corby Distilleries: Wiser's; Craigellachie Distillery; Cragganmore Distillery; Des Menhirs: Eddu; Diageo plc: Bell's, Black & White, Buchanan's, Bulleit Bourbon, Bushmills, Cameron Brig, Caol Ila, Cardhu, Crown Royal, Dalwhinnie, Dimple, Glen Elgin, Haig, J&B, Johnnie Walker, Lagavulin, Linkwood, Oban, Old Parr, Royal Lochnagar, Teaninich, Usher's Green Stripe, VAT 69, White Horse, Windsor; Diageo Canada: Seagram's; Domaine Charbay: Charbay; Domaine Mavela: P&M; Edrington Group: The Famous Grouse, Tamdhu; The English Whisky Co.; Fleischmann: Grüner Hund; Four Roses Distillery; The Gaelic Whisky Co.: Poit Dhubh; George A. Dickel & Co.: George Dickel; Girvan Distillery; Glencadam Distillery; Glendronach Distillery; Glendullan Distillery; Glenfarclas Distillery; Glenfiddich Distillery; Glenglassaugh Distillery; Glengoyne Distillery; Glenkinchie Distillery; Glenlivet Distillery; The Glenmorangie Company: Bailie Nicol Jarvie, Glenmorangie, James Martin's; Glenora Distillery: Glen Breton; Glenrothes Distillery; Glenturret Distillery; Graanstokerij Filliers: Goldlys; Great Southern Distilling Company: Limeburners; Guillon Distillery; Heaven Hill Distilleries, Inc.: Bernheim, Elijah Craig, Evan Williams, Heaven Hill, Georgia Moon, Mellow Corn, Old Fitzgerald, Parker's, Pikesville, Rittenhouse Rye; Highland Park Distillery; Highwood Distillers; Holle; Ian MacLeod: Langs; International Beverage Holdings; Inver House Distillers: Catto's, Hankey Bannister, Inver House, MacArthur's, Pinwinnie Royale, Speyburn; Isle of Arran: Robert Burns; Jura Distillery; Käsers Schloss: Whisky Castle; Kentucky Bourbon Distillers, Ltd.: Johnny Drum; Kilchoman Distillery; King Car Whisky Distillery: Kavalan; Kirin Holdings Company; Kittling Ridge Distillery: Forty Creek; Knockdhu Distillery: AnCnoc; Knockeen Hills; La Maison du Whisky: Nikka; Lark Distillery; Last Drop Distillers; Luxco Spirited Brands: Rebel Yell; Macallan; Macduff International: Grand Macnish, Islay Mist, Lauder's; Mackmyra; McMenamin's Group: Edgefield; Midleton Distillery: Clontarf, Crested Ten, Dungourney, Green Spot, The Irishman, Jameson, Midleton, Paddy, Powers, Redbreast, Tullamore Dew; Morrison Bowmore Distillers: Auchentoshan, Bowmore, Glen Garioch, McClelland's, Yamazaki; Murree Distillery; The Nant Estate; The New Zealand Malt Whisky Company: Milford; The Nikka Whisky Distilling Co.; Number One Drinks Company: Chichibu, Hanyu, Ichiro's Malt; Old Pulteney Distillery; The Owl Distillery: The Belgian Owl; Pernod Ricard USA: American Spirit, Russell's Reserve, Wild Turkey; Piedmont Distillers: Catdaddy; Preiss Imports; Radico Khaitan: 8PM; Reisetbauer; Richard Joynson: Loch Fyne; Rogue Spirits; Rosebank Distillery; Saint James Spirits: Peregrine Rock; Sazerac Company, Inc.: Ancient Age, Blanton's, Buffalo Trace, Eagle Rare, Elmer T. Lee, Experimental Collection, George T. Stagg, Hancock's Reserve, Kentucky Gentleman, Old Charter, Ridgemont, Sazerac Rye, Thomas H. Handy, W.L. Weller, Very Old Barton; Scapa Distillery; Spencerfield Spirits: Pig's Nose; Speyside Distillery; Springbank Distillers: Hazelburn, Longrow, Springbank; St George Spirits; Stock Plzen: Printer's; Stranahan's Colorado Whiskey; Suntory Group; Tasmania Distillery: Sullivan's Cove; Teerenpeli; Templeton Rye; Talisker Distillery; Tobermory Distillery: Ledaig, Tobermory; Tomatin Distillery: The Antiquary, Tomatin; Tomintoul Distillery; Triple Eight Distillery: The Notch; Tullibardine Distillery; Tuthilltown Distillery: Hudson; United Spirits; Us Heit Distillery: Frysk Hynder; Waldviertler Whiskydestillerie; Wambrechies Distillery; Welsh Whisky Company: Penderyn; Whyte & Mackay: Black Dog, The Claymore, Cluny, The Dalmore, Tamnavulin, Whyte & Mackay; William Grant & Sons: Clan MacGregor, Glenfiddich, Grant's, Ladyburn, Monkey Shoulder; Zuidam Distillery: Millstone.

Additional studio and location photography by Chris Bunting (Golden Horse 163), The Whisky Couple (Wild Turkey sign 230, Maker's Mark 231), and The Whisky Exchange (Hirsch Reserve 183). All other images by Thameside Media/Michael Ellis © DK Images.

Jacket images: (top row, left to right) Nikka Yoichi 10-year-old, Seagram's VO, The Famous Grouse Gold Reserve 12-year-old, Redbreast 12-year-old, Kirin Gotemba Fujisanroku 18-year-old, Dimple 12-year-old, Wild Turkey 80 Proof; (bottom row, left to right) Glenfiddich 12-year-old, Old Potrero, George Dickel No.12, Black Dog Centenary, Jameson Special Reserve 12-year-old, Jura 10-year-old, The Glenlivet XXV.